# THE BUSINESS OF SHOW

## A Guide to the Entertainment Business for the Performing Artist

## ADAM CATES

*Foreword by*

Michael Cassara, CSA

www.businessofshow.info

Library of Congress Control Number: 2014913274

CreateSpace Independent Publishing Platform, North Charleston, SC

ISBN: 1499236417
ISBN-13: 978-1499236415

# DEDICATION

To my students (past, present, and future) who inspired me to write this in the first place, this is for you. May you find the answers you seek and happy fulfilling lives both in and out of the performing arts.

To my family and loved ones who offered guidance, lent support, or read one manuscript after the next, I am forever grateful. Steve Saari, Roy Lightner, Venita McLemore, Cassie Abate, Peggy Hickey, Rachel Anderson, and my parents Dick and Jane Cates, I love you and I thank you for supporting my dreams. To my esteemed colleague and friend, Michael Cassara, thank you for your contributions not only to this book but also to my career over the years.

To my niece and nephew, Stephanie and Tony Caramella, always be who you want to be! And if you should happen to go into show business, well, keep this book with you and call me a lot.

# Special Thanks & Acknowledgments

The joy-filled process of creating this book has allowed me to reconnect with many amazing and inspiring artists from across my life and career.

These are the mentors, friends, and colleagues who generously contributed the stories, advice, pet peeves, guidance, and truths that made this project a reality. May this help our next generation of artists achieve the same dreams we have. Thank you all from the bottom of my heart. I am grateful.

Cassie Abate, Gary Aldrich, Clyde Alves, Timothy George Anderson, Maud Arnold, Nura Awda, Dan Barris, Judy Blazer, Pamela Bob, Amy Bodnar, Troy Edward Bowles, Justin Brill, Wayne Bryan, Haven Burton, Stephen Carrasco, Michael Cassara, John Charron, Mark Chmiel, Patti Colombo, Jonathan Corella-Sandler, Kristen Coury, Nicholas Cunningham, Seán Curran, Joshua Dean, Stephen DeRosa, Lucille DiCampli, Kurt Domoney, Michelle Dyer, Eric Sean Fogel, Jacki Dowling Ford, Dexter Foxworth, Ben Franklin, Crystal Frazier, Karla Garcia, Jason Graae, Justin Greer, Mark Hansen, Peggy Hickey, Richard J. Hinds, Anne Horak, Kate Hutter, Alex Isbell, Danielle Jordan, R. Kim Jordan, Gus Kaikkonen, Naomi Kakuk, Jinger Leigh-Kalin, Christine Kerber, Matthew Kiernan, Bruce Kimmel, Ian Knauer, Dan Kolodny, Erica Hartono Kolodny, Kenway Kua, Phil LaDuca, Lisa Lehr, Jeremy Leiner, Matt Lenz, Roy Lightner, Constantine Maroulis, Ellyn Marie Marsh, Kathleen Marshall, Evan Tyrone Martin, Philip Wm. McKinley, Sean McKnight, Venita McLemore, Lauren Molina, Linda Mugleston, Denny Paschall, Liz Pearce, Barry Pearl, Dante Puleio, Angel Reed, Jay Russell, David Ruttura, William Ryall, Steve Saari, Tommy Scrivens, Amy Jo Slater, Yvette Tucker Spencer, Janelle Abbott Staley, Tracie Stanfield, Leslie Stevens, Jodie Stinebaugh, Mic Thompson, Jamie Torcellini, Christine Townsend, Shanna Vanderwerker, Wes Veldink, Jessica Walter, Anthony Wayne, Randal K. West

# CONTENTS

# Foreword

On my office bookshelf there are two well-worn editions that have survived many years and many moves. One is Fred Silver's *Auditioning for the Musical Theatre*; the other is Michael Shurtleff's *Audition.* In the pre-Google era during which I grew up and pursued a career as a performer, those books were my lifelines to the world of professional theatre: its glamour, its exacting standards, and its joy. I found myself bringing them along with me on summer stock contracts and regional theatre jobs, but ultimately they would find a more permanent home on the bookshelf of the theatrical casting office I opened in midtown Manhattan.

In those books, the authors (both revered theatrical artists themselves) attempted to demystify the audition process and help performers understand what goes into the casting process of a professional theatrical production. While both books remain invaluable and remarkable, our industry has changed in many profound ways since their publication leaving a great void for today's aspiring theatre artists in search of guidance.

With *The Business of Show*, Adam Cates has filled that void by offering the 21st Century performer a practical and powerful guide to navigating the murky-but-majestic waters of our beloved industry.

As a casting director, I have a unique vantage point. I get to watch thousands of auditions every year. I'd venture to say there's very little I haven't seen in the audition room (though, as they say, "Just when you think you've seen it all...."") and, while much of what I witness is inspiring, entertaining, or profound, much more of it is none of those things. How I wish every performer would read this book and take its lessons to heart before auditioning for me.

Today's performers must be versatile and ready for anything. With so much information available to them, and with such intense competition surrounding them, I'm all the more thrilled by this concise guidebook and the accessible manner in which it illuminates the steps one must take to begin a sustainable career in the arts.

As I read the anecdotes of many colleagues and friends who are quoted, I noticed some commonalities. They are practical and compassionate, sage and energetic. Adam assembled a diverse array of top theatre practitioners and encouraged them to be honest. Ours is a bipolar industry—stability is not a frequent visitor in our field, yet every year there are busloads of newly arriving artists who *do* find a way to earn a living in the arts. With careful attention to the specifics herein, one might end up among their ranks.

It would seem to me that more people are pursuing performance careers than ever before. Certainly, there are more training programs (with more offering New York and Los Angeles senior showcase presentations) than there were just 10 years ago. My office often holds open call auditions where we see 400 people in a single day and *still* don't get to audition everyone who would like to be seen. Suffice it to say, show business will not be getting easier anytime soon. In the coming pages, however, many opportunities within the entertainment industry are examined including many that exist beyond just performance opportunities. I encourage you to soak it all up and explore every option you possibly can.

To carve out a life in the entertainment industry, one must have thick skin and a dedicated drive, however, one must also have knowledge— fortunately, a great deal of knowledge can be found in *The Business of Show*. I found myself nodding in agreement as I turned every page. Adam Cates is one of my favorite collaborators. He is as giving as he is talented, which has never been on display more engagingly than in the volume you are about to read. And, just as the words of Mr. Shurtleff and Mr. Silver brilliantly served a generation of Broadway hopefuls, I am confident this book will offer a vital lifeline for the next busload of Broadway greats.

Michael Cassara, CSA
New York, NY
July, 2014

**Michael Cassara, CSA** is a casting director and educator based in New York City. Since the formation of Michael Cassara Casting in 2003, he and his team have cast over 300 theatre and film projects, and currently serve as the resident casting office for both the New York Musical Theatre Festival (NYMF) and the National Alliance for Musical Theatre (NAMT). A native Clevelander, Michael holds a BFA in musical theatre from Otterbein College (now Otterbein University) and has taught musical theatre auditioning and "the business of the business" at dozens of top universities and training programs throughout the U.S. and worldwide. He is a member of the Casting Society of America. Please visit www.michaelcassara.net and "follow" him on Facebook and Twitter: @MichaelCassara.

THE BUSINESS OF SHOW

# INTRODUCTION

# It's Called Show "Business"

*There's no business like show business*
*Like no business I know*
*Everything about it is appealing*
*Everything that traffic will allow*
*Nowhere could you get that happy feeling*
*When you are stealing that extra bow*

*There's no people like show people*
*They smile when they are low*
*Even with a turkey that you know will fold*
*You may be stranded out in the cold*
*Still you wouldn't change it for a sack of gold*
*Let's go on with the show*

*There's no business like show business*
*Like no business I know*
*You get word before the show has started*
*That your favorite uncle died at dawn*
*Top of that, your pa and ma have parted*
*You're broken-hearted, but you go on*

*There's no people like show people*
*They smile when they are low*
*Yesterday they told you you would not go far*
*That night you open and there you are*
*Next day on your dressing room*
*They've hung a star*
*Let's go, on with the show*

**-Irving Berlin**

The iconic lyrics from Irving Berlin's song "There's No Business Like Show Business," from the 1946 Broadway musical *Annie Get Your Gun*, still capture the spirit, the sacrifices, the passion, the heartache, and the triumph that contribute to a career as a performing artist. There is nothing quite like the feeling of performing in front of a captive audience. Realizing there is a possibility to make an actual living from performing can be profound for a young artist. Ah, the allure of "show business"—but one must remember that the phrase has two parts. A love for the "show" is probably why you picked up this book. The "business" is what you need to learn from it. This book is not about the craft of performing (that would be the "show" part, the talent, the technique, "the work"), but rather the ins and outs of "the business"—the other work one must do to accomplish a professional career as a performing artist.

### Before we begin, you need to accept, know, and understand these three things.

First, the road to success for a professional performer is hard, bumpy, and painful. This is true for *everyone*, no matter where you come from or how good you are. There. I said it, and it's the real truth. Success will seem arbitrary. No one simply "deserves it." If you want a career based on "fairness," then this is not it. Success doesn't find people just because they want it to. And that's the first thing you need to accept.

Second, you are likely reading this book because you have dreams. You've been dancing since age three, you've loved performing "forever," or you recently discovered that theater is your calling. You want to perform on Broadway, or tour with Beyoncé, or star on a TV series. Those dreams can be realistic—why not? Real people like you book those jobs every day and achieve those goals. Your dreams could be next. Embrace that optimism. The second thing to know is that you have the right to pursue your dream.

The third and most important thing you have to understand is that dreaming alone won't get you that job. The jobs you want require not just great talent but a successful navigation of "the business." The business can be extremely rewarding one day but also unforgiving, heartbreaking, and at times terrifying the next. This is true for every performer regardless of success or stature—professional show business is not the right path for every talented individual because a love of performing is not enough. The

old adage is true: If you could love any other career just as mu
than performing, you should strongly consider pursuing that
Dedicating your life and *livelihood* to the arts is a different gam
fulfilling your desire to perform. Pursuing other interests doesn't mean you
have to dismiss your passion for the arts. You can perform with community
theaters and find inspiration watching professional performances while
achieving another career with passion and greater stability. People choose
this path all the time. Think about the kind of life you really want.

Did I scare you off?

Oh, you're still reading. Well, great—read on because, in truth, you
just might be one of us!

People who pursue the arts as a profession do so because they *have* to.
They are compelled—the mind, body, and soul can imagine no other life.
They face head on the sacrifices, hard times and hard work. They want it
more than anything else.

As luck would have it, we are a nation full of talented artists and, more
important, extremely gifted teachers. The United States has a wealth of
performing arts conservatories, university training programs, and
exceptional hometown vocal, dance, and theater studios where students can
develop incredible technique, artistry, and performance skills. Opportunities
exist. While artistic training for performers is widely accessible, the
schooling in the business side of the profession is somewhat rare. Thus, the
idea for this book! The business of show is its own beast and though early
navigation isn't easy, this book may help start you off on the right foot.

### Here is what this book WILL NOT do:

It won't give you more talent. It won't make you a better dancer, singer, or
actor. It won't increase your range. It won't give you tips on how to land
that triple turn every time or pick up choreography faster. It won't help you
hit that higher note or find the emotional arc of your character. It won't
even make you better at the act of auditioning. Those are the things you
must learn in your study of the art form. If you want to be a professional
performing artist, then get into class like it's your job—listen to your
teachers, embody corrections, strengthen your core, delve deeper, jump

.er, turn better, sing stronger, and sweat until you think you might pass
.ut! Do these things every day!!! Become the absolute best you can be and
do it now. Go for it and get good. *Now!* I guarantee that the person
auditioning next to you is doing it, so, what are *you* waiting for?

## Here is what this book WILL do:

It will help you acquire the essential business tools for presenting your best
professional self. It will explain the process of pursuing work. It will teach
you industry lingo, introduce available resources, highlight types of jobs and
where the work is, and show how agents and unions can be a part of your
career. It will give you a better understanding of the expectations once
you've booked a job and ways to grow your career from one job to the
next. You might be in your late teens or early 20s and ready both technically
and artistically to begin working professionally. I want to help you become
a more informed professional and avoid learning lessons the hard way.
Choosing to make a living as a performer doesn't mean you are required to
sign up for a life of poverty and debt (despite what some well-meaning but
excusably uninformed people in your life may have told you!). Making wise
business decisions early on can set you up for success as you grow.

I'm proof that it's possible. No one in my family had ever worked in
the professional entertainment industry before me. Growing up, my family
was certainly supportive of my love for dance and theater, taking me to
class, paying the fees, attending my shows, and driving me around the
country for competitions. But when I decided to pursue a career as a
performing artist, they didn't have the answers to guide me down a
particular path. How could I have expected them to? I grew up in Reno,
Nevada. It wasn't a large city, but it did have a thriving professional
entertainment scene during my childhood in the 1970s, '80s, and '90s. I was
lucky to have some incredible teachers who gave me solid training, inspired
my artistic passion, and helped guide me toward a career. I had
opportunities to get my professional feet wet as a teen in the Reno/Lake
Tahoe area. I opted for college and earned my bachelor of arts in theater
from the University of Utah.

After performing regionally for a couple years in theme parks, summer
stock, casino revues, and cruise lines, I made the big move to New York
City to further my career. The first couple years were really hard, but

eventually I found my niche working as a performer, choreographer, and director on national tours, television series, off-Broadway theater, industrials, operas, and dance convention tours; on projects in Los Angeles, New York, Las Vegas, and Europe; at big and small regional and stock theaters; and even on Broadway (my dream!). I have been fortunate to live the life I dreamt about as a kid! My career hasn't been all ups with no downs—it continues to involve hard work—but I learned early on, from great mentors and my own mishaps, ways to navigate and find an understanding of the business end. You can too.

The professional opinions in these pages are not just my own. I have sought the expertise of a variety of professionals, including seasoned performers who have worked successfully across every medium. Here you'll find real-world information directly from working directors, choreographers, producers, casting directors, agents, college professors, and other experts who each began with a dream similar to yours. Not every person is a household name, but each has developed and sustained a career in the performing arts over a decade or more. These colleagues were all eager to offer their advice, stories, suggestions, and insight to help you pursue your dreams. Take it all in. Make use of the "business slang" footnotes throughout the book to learn or clarify the terminology that may be new to you. I hope that you find this book to be a helpful tool. Merde![1]

Let's get started…

---

[1] Merde: a traditional term meaning "good luck" usually used by dancers prior to a performance, similar to saying "break a leg." In French, it literally means "shit." There are various theories on how this tradition originated; however, we know it began during the early period of opera/ballet in Paris.

# Chapter One

# Training

If performing (dancing, singing, acting) is "your life" and you are hoping to make a career of it, the first essential step to becoming a professional is to focus on your training. It doesn't matter if you have been singing on stage since you were age three or just started dance classes at age 18; the time to dive into rigorous training is now. Find the best teachers you can find. Don't limit yourself. Push yourself to become the best you can be. The yearning to refine and better your craft must be strong within you, or else this career is honestly not for you.

## HIGHER EDUCATION

Most jobs, careers, and trades require some sort of study beyond high school through an institute of higher education. Why should a career in the arts be any different? The entertainment world is a multibillion-dollar industry, and success requires preparedness and skill.

You may already be immersed in your chosen training program. That's great news! If you have not yet figured out where to study, you have some decisions to make. There are a few different paths of formal artistic education most performers choose from. Explore them all to find the one that is right for you.

### UNIVERSITY, COLLEGE, & CONSERVATORY DEGREES

Many state and private universities and colleges offer degrees in theater, voice, or dance. There was a time in academia when the trend was to prepare students only to teach in the arts. This focus still exists as an option; however, the last 30 years have seen a national shift in focus, with more programs geared toward performers hoping to enter the commercial entertainment profession. In a university or college bachelors program, you will receive some type of liberal arts education in addition to studying in your chosen major. University degrees offered are a bachelor of arts, bachelor of music, or a bachelor of science. At community and junior colleges you can earn an associates degree. Masters degrees exist beyond that. Some university programs are even further focused toward a specific genre or medium. These conservatory degree programs are more concentrated and don't always include liberal arts requirements not directly related to one's chosen field. Conservatory programs offered through a university award a bachelor of fine arts or music. University bachelor degree programs on average take four years to complete. Junior colleges average roughly two years to earn an associates degree, and depending on the state system, your classes can be applied toward a bachelors degree should you further matriculate at a university. Continuing on to earn a master of fine arts or music degree could take another one to three years.

The level to which you attain your degree of training is up to you. Some people study in a program but leave to enter the profession before they are finished. You don't get the maximum benefit of the program that way, but to some it doesn't matter. Singers pursuing opera performance tend to complete a bachelors and then an MFA or equivalent before entering the industry through apprentice and young artists programs. Singers pursuing musical theater only sometimes pursue a masters. Many bachelors degrees specific to musical theater do an excellent job of preparing students to work within four years. Dancers who pursue a masters after obtaining a bachelors generally do so only if they intend to teach or want to pursue choreography, but there are some great MFAs in dance performance out there too. Theater majors may find bachelors options in general theater or performance.

Focused actor training programs tend to be BFA programs. Actors might pursue a masters degree if they want to further develop skills in classical styles like Shakespeare or hone skills in a specific technique. Some prestigious MFA acting programs have high percentages of alumni who have found success. Sometimes performers earn a bachelors degree from a university and then go on to study in a professional studio program, which we'll discuss next. It is rare for performers to pursue a doctorate degree, or

PhD, prior to beginning a professional performance career. Usually those performers with PhDs have pursued them when transitioning away from performing and onto a new path.

Peggy Hickey, a Los Angeles-based choreographer, MTV Video Music Award winner, and faculty member of UCLA's Ray Bolger musical theater program, continues to choreograph for Broadway, major opera companies, regional theaters, and network television. She sees hundreds of new professionals at auditions each year. She advises:

> *The best-prepared performers are the ones coming out of good college programs. Degrees used to not mean much professionally. I came out of a college program, and I was no more prepared to find work, get work or even know what kind of performer I was than I was prepared to fly. It's different now. College programs are better. The new breed of kids with degrees is much more supercharged; they know how to dress, they know how to sing, they know what to expect in the audition room. They understand auditioning as a skill, and have a better understanding of the system.*

Regional theater director/choreographer and Texas State University professor Cassie Abate further explains:

> *This is a business where there is no one path. Everyone has a completely different journey. There are those few incredibly talented individuals who "make it" right out of high school. However, I don't think that is the norm and I would highly recommend that a person go to college. I think they have a better chance of succeeding after having four years to develop not only as an artist, but also as a person. You gain the skills to use your talents to their best ability. You also learn technique and stamina that will help you maintain a long and healthy career. Finally, the people you go to school with will be the next generation of performers, directors, choreographers, casting directors, producers, etc.*

I won't attempt to list the popular opinions of which schools are the top or best schools—those statistics change often as new people start programs and old people leave, and discovering that information should be a part of the research you need to learn to do on your own. There are many schools to choose from and all offer different philosophies of training. If your high school counselor or family is not familiar with specific programs that match your talent, needs and goals, they may not know how best to guide you. So, it's on you to figure it out. Take the bull by the horns, get on the Internet, and start "Googling." Trade websites, including BroadwayWorld.com, and publications, such as *Dance Magazine*, publish listings of training programs across the country. How will you know which one is the right school for you? I can't tell you that, nor can anyone else. You know you best. But you can begin to narrow down your search by making the following lists. (No, really, get out a piece of paper and make these lists. I'm going to ask you to do this a lot. I promise it will help...)

✓ Ask your dance and drama teachers, community theater directors, vocal coaches, and master guest teachers what schools they think you should research. Professionals who know your strengths and interests who have knowledge of programs out there will have good suggestions.

✓ Where did the performers you admire go to school? When looking at school websites, find the alumni lists and see what work program graduates have gone on to do. Is the alumni association active in relation to the program? This may give you advantages upon graduation.

✓ Conservatory programs and university liberal arts education programs differ in what they require, and you should decide which is a better fit for you. Do you want a well-rounded, diverse education from a university or do you want an extremely concentrated course of study from a conservatory?

✓ Whom do you want to study with? Read the faculty bios to discover who has a background in the field you hope to pursue. Is it important to you that faculty members are still actively working in the industry?

✓ Learn what opportunities a program offers that makes it special or unique. How many and what types of performance opportunities are available to students? Does the school have any associations with professional theater, dance, or opera companies? Who has come in to conduct master classes or residencies? Do graduating seniors perform a showcase in New York, Chicago, or Los Angeles for agents, casting directors, or producers?

✓ Are you interested in a specialized program? Most schools offer degrees in theater, music, or dance, but some offer focused degrees in commercial dance, musical theater, acting for film, opera performance, ballet, modern dance, or choreography. Research what the differences are and which might best serve your personal goals.

✓ How are your academic grades and standardized test scores? Universities will require that you meet admission standards for acceptance first before being accepted into a degree program; however, some conservatories might not. Find out all the specifics.

✓ Where is the school located? How many people do they accept into a program each year? Can you transfer in from another school? Is on-campus housing available? What are the costs, and can you apply for financial awards like scholarships or grants? Will you need to apply for student loans? Can you participate in a work/study program to help defray costs?

✓ Competitive programs only accept a limited number of incoming and/or transfer students. Students are selected through an audition process. Department websites will generally list information regarding local auditions and many universities also participate in audition conferences where you can be seen by many schools at once. National Unified Auditions (www.unifiedauditions.com) holds regional audition conferences for schools each year.

These important factors carry different weight and naturally affect final decisions. The good news is there are many great training programs across the United States and abroad. You have options. Narrow your search down, but don't limit yourself to just a single choice. Should you not get in to your top school, it is wise to have backup choices. If you have the means, I advise you to contact and physically visit your top choices. A program advisor can help you coordinate your visit. Ask to meet current students, see a student production, talk with the department advisor, and sit in on a class. Find out if there are auditions for specific degree programs, and when they are. Do they have a summer intensive you can attend? By the time you have compared your visits, the schools that feel right to you will become obvious.

Just like any profession, having your bachelors degree in hand does not write your ticket to a successful career as a performer. A bachelors degree itself won't necessarily change anyone's mind about you as they watch your audition for their show. What having a bachelors degree means is that you have invested valuable time into the training necessary to better your artistry. Having a degree will open doors for you in other ways throughout your life. Going to college will not hurt you.

## PROFESSIONAL STUDIO & CONSERVATORY PROGRAMS

Let's face it, not everyone has the means or a desire to continue with a formal university education after high school. That's okay. Not going to college doesn't mean you can't "make it" in show business. There are performers who graduate from high school, move to New York or L.A., and start working professionally right away without an additional period of training. In today's industry this would account for a small and exceptional percentage of professionals. Chances are these individuals already began a professional career before graduating high school. Foregoing college and moving to a major city is not necessarily the easiest path, but most of the successful ones who have foregone a college education have not ignored their advanced training. Regardless of work, continuing education for a young adult artist *in some way* should be a priority. Your colleagues around you (auditioning next to you!) will be extremely well trained, and if you want to keep up, training is essential.

In major markets like New York, Los Angeles, Chicago, and some others, as an alternative to a four-year university degree, there exist accredited vocal, theater, film, comedy improv, and dance studios and conservatories for professional artists that offer full-time and part-time intensive degree or certificate programs. Professional dance, opera, and acting companies may have a school attached that allows for students to segue into a professional contract with the company. These conservatory training programs may be non-degree yet prestigious and respected in the industry. Scholarships, work/study, and/or apprenticeships are available in most cases as are connections to school alumni. Studio and conservatory programs can vary in length from six months to two years and may offer the same type of showcase opportunity as a university does. They provide a concentrated course of study without the academic requirements. Many performers find these options more appealing.

The type of education that is most useful may differ in some markets depending on what kind of work you want to pursue. Studying with a specialized studio may be a better answer in certain commercial fields. As you continue to decide what part of the industry and/or market you want to pursue, you need to evaluate what you feel is the best fit for you. Wes Veldink, a commercial and concert dance choreographer as well as creative director, used to teach for the EDGE Performing Arts Center Scholarship Program, a professional studio that has served as a launch pad for the careers of many commercial dancers in Los Angeles. Wes graduated high school from the Orange County School for the Performing Arts, jumped successfully into the L.A. market immediately following, and landed dance roles in films such as *Newsies* and videos for Paula Abdul and Michael Jackson.

*LA is such a free-for-all. Busloads of dancers, actors, and singers are showing up every day and it's just a big pool of talent. I remember back in high school understanding that I could go to college, but then would graduate and be in exactly the same place with everybody else: auditioning. And the choreographers wouldn't care that I had a degree, only that I had the talent and the look they wanted. In the early 1990s, most college programs prepared you for later down the road when you wanted to teach or work in a related field, but at the time it wasn't so much a segue into the work as a professional dancer.*

Research studios and conservatories with the same checklist you used to learn about university options. Trade magazines frequently run ads that aid in finding these schools. Competitive professional studios will also require you to audition, as they only accept a limited number of new students per term.

## LOCAL ALTERNATIVES

If you don't live in a city with a known professional studio, don't have the means to move to a big city just yet, or aren't able to attend college for financial reasons, you aren't without options. Take advantage of whatever training is available in your hometown community. Is there a professional dance company with a school where you can take weekly classes? Has a retired singer opened a vocal studio? Is there a professional theater company looking to hire local production assistants or actors, even if they are nonpaid? Seek out every opportunity your community has to offer and don't limit yourself. Look into summer intensive programs where you can study in residence. Some may require you to travel, but will offer you an outside perspective and broaden your knowledge.

Be wary of the teachers who insist on total exclusivity. Though the knowledge and training they offer might be great, an educator who prioritizes his or her students' needs understands that students grow exponentially when given the opportunity to learn from multiple perspectives. Don't allow yourself be limited by those who "won't allow you" to study with other teachers. Dan Barris, the owner and founder of Dancers Inc. conventions, provides students in cities across the country the opportunity to work directly with professional master teachers from New York and L.A.

> *My kids have always been encouraged to study with multiple teachers because it gives them a step up in the industry. You are never going to walk into an audition and see your teacher standing in front of you. If you only study with one teacher you will only be used to one style of learning material. Take classes from teachers you don't know so that you have the ability to walk into an audition room cold. The reinforcement you receive in class, both positive and negative, will help you hone your audition skills.*

## SCAM SCHOOLS

Ever hear the phrase "If it sounds too good to be true, it probably is"? Don't believe everything you hear without also fact-checking for yourself. Unfortunately, there are plenty of people out there who are more than willing to take advantage of a naïve student with stars in his or her eyes. There are "schools" or teachers who make promises of instant stardom and guarantees that you'll sign with a big agency or get a film deal if you study with them—for a price....

Did you know that if you say the word *gullible* out loud really slowly, it sounds like the word *orange?*

You tried it, didn't you…. Lesson learned: be wary of someone else's scam.

If you come across a school that interests you, my advice is that you do your research. Get on the Internet and check out what is being said about the school or teacher. Successful and legitimate schools tend to have a public track record somewhere online. Don't take just one person's word for it. Ask professionals what they know. Find out if the school is accredited or not. Research it with the same checklist you would use to find out about a university or conservatory. If you are going to pay money for training, you should learn from people or an institution with a proven body of work and a reputation that can be backed up. If you have doubts about a school's legitimacy, it is probably not the right school for you. The more you get into this book, the more you will learn that those promises of fame and fortune from any school are empty guarantees.

## "WAIT AND SEE WHAT HAPPENS" IS NOT A PLAN

In the end, some form of higher training is better than no further training. I have never met a performer just graduating high school who wouldn't benefit from continued education in their early adult years, college or not. Study. The worst thing you can do is to just wait to "see what happens." I have talked to students over the years whose plan is to attend an audition after graduation for an agent, or job, or company and then just wait and "see what happens" after that. I can tell you with certainty that what will happen is nothing. The people who find success are the people who go after it. You must have ambition, and you must be the one who proactively seeks out multiple opportunities if your goal is to achieve a career. Putting all your eggs in one basket and then waiting for someone else to pick that basket up and carry it is not going to lead you to success. Making your education a priority is a step in the right direction.

# OWN YOUR TRAINING

In the end, whether you go to college or a conservatory or other training program beyond high school, you must remember that becoming a professional is not a race. New York will still be there when you are ready. Los Angeles will still be there when you are ready. Get your training first and then get into your market of choice. Our industry is not dying—great jobs will be available when you are truly ready to take on a career.

Professional training programs will offer specific advisement, but ultimately, it is *you* who are responsible for your training. You must own your decisions and chart your own progress. You must gauge your own preparedness and work ethic. Undoubtedly, you will have questions. Some that are frequently asked include:

**"I'm in school. Now what do I do?"**

Study. Commit. Get to class. Audition for department productions. Perform whenever you can and keep your training as your top priority. Every program is going to have a rigorous schedule of requirements you will have to meet in order to graduate, and hopefully you are being offered a well-rounded curriculum. That doesn't mean, however, that you should let someone else have control. You are in charge of your education. Some classes you need might be outside the structure of your major. Talk to your advisor about getting into those classes and get the training that will help you to succeed. (You are paying for it after all!) If you are majoring in dance and want to pursue musical theater professionally, but your degree program does not require that you take voice and acting classes, you must take it upon yourself to find and enroll in those classes! You need them. If you are an actor or singer who has taken the required number of dance classes but still cannot pick up choreography or move with fluidity, sign up for more! You need them. These additional classes may fulfill another general education requirement or they may not. That doesn't matter. Your skill level is what matters. You say, "But I don't have time!" What!? Make time. Enough with the excuses! If setting yourself up to succeed is as important as you claim it is, you will make the time in your schedule. Priorities, priorities, priorities....

**"My parents think I should major in something else to fall back on. Should I?"**

I hear this a lot. Yes, a career in the arts is difficult and not everyone "makes it," so majoring in something else to fall back on in case it doesn't work out seems like a smart option, right? Even my own parents hoped I

would do that. (And I did—for one whole semester! Political science was a bust...my heart was somewhere else.)

True, a career in the arts is unpredictable. But if you know performing is what you want to do, let's take a look at the reality: The job market for any young adult is rough, and any professional career, no matter what it may be, is going to be hard, competitive, and requiring of great effort. That's our world—those factors aren't unique to performing artists. If you wanted a career as a doctor, would your parents encourage you to major in English literature just in case you didn't get into medical school? I'm going to venture the answer is "no." You'd major in pre-med or a related science so you *could* get into medical school! If your driving passion were to become a kindergarten teacher, would you do better to spend four years studying business or education and child development? If it makes sense to major appropriately for other industries, the same holds true for ours. Get that training. Get exceptionally good at what you want to do. Set yourself up for success! Your four years in college are your most crucial years of training—use that time wisely. Believe that you can succeed and take that positive energy with you into your career. Majoring in something else because you are afraid of failure is unhealthy—how do you intend to "confidently" begin a career that way?

On the flip side, there are some people who major in something else not because of a fear of failure but because they are truly interested in also learning about something else. Some people double major in their art and another subject. That's totally different. That's another case of you needing to know yourself, what you want, and what you can handle. Getting a degree in another subject because it interests you and majoring in something else because you think you will fail at your dream are not the same things. You may double major and find that you can combine your love of the performing arts with education, development, therapy, or arts management. There are vast opportunities out there beyond just performing, and college is another chance for you to explore your interests.

If your goal is to perform professionally, at the end of the day you will either graduate with the training you need to get a career started or you won't. You make that choice for yourself; no one else is responsible for your training but you. Regardless of your major, if you want a career as a performer, you need to hone your craft. In today's market, you must be well studied and prepared. "Natural" talent is simply not enough....

**"I know I need more training, but I would rather just dive into the work."**

Maybe you are the one who is ready to start working right out of high school. I don't know you.... But don't be so quick to write off further education. Consider that there may be options for you to train and work at the same time. If you choose a college, conservatory, or studio that is connected to a professional company, there could be opportunities to take your classes and also perform as a non-union apprentice in professional productions at the same time. Are you living in a community with a professional dinner theater? Go to school during the day and audition for the jobs that perform at night. Singers might have the option of performing in concerts with local symphonies and chorales. If you are in a university program, consider that you have the summer months free. Audition for summer stock companies or theme parks—jobs that exist on a seasonal schedule. Track down a local casting agency and audition for the occasional film, TV, or commercial work that may arise in your area.

By doing all of these things, you can gain valuable work experience and possibly make some money. When I went to college in Salt Lake City, I found myself on film sets and Equity stages as often as I found myself involved in department productions. I didn't have to choose between training and getting my professional feet wet. The opportunities are out there—make it a point to understand the region you live in and the available job opportunities. Building a resume while also pursuing an education gives you the best of both worlds. You can supplement your education and have a leg up when you eventually enter the work force full-time.

**"What if I am not sure I want to perform for the rest of my**

There is a lot of pressure on high school and college students to p. lifelong career path *right now*. That pressure is not necessarily fair. No one has to decide his or her whole life's path right now. Adults change careers all the time, no matter what field they work in or what degree they attained. I know several people who got degrees in theater or dance, had successful careers as performers throughout early adulthood, and then decided it was time to do something else. They went back to school to become doctors, lawyers, or small business owners, etc., and now they are successful doctors, lawyers, or small business owners, etc. You'll read about a few of them later.

Some people are born to work in show business forever. Some are not. You don't have to know that about yourself *right now*—life will lead you to that answer. But if you know that for now you want to pursue a professional career, go for it! It is a journey you need to embark on as a young adult. People don't decide to start dancing professionally in their 40s. That is not a reality. If you are going to do it, do it now and prepare yourself to be successful.

# VERSATILITY IS KEY

Even though your most developed talent may be concentrated in one medium, many working professionals will tell you that your early training for a career should include *everything*! What they mean is that diversity of skill will serve you much more than being good at just one thing. Don't just dabble in other skill sets—really study, really practice, really get good! If you possess multiple skills that you can do well, you'll be right for a larger percentage of jobs. Not much can be done with a "one-trick pony"—it will limit you. For example, if you *only* tap dance, you will be capable of booking jobs that *only* need tap dancers. The market is more diverse than that. What about the job that needs tap dancers who also have legitimate ballet technique? Without the ballet technique, it won't matter what your tap skills are—they can't use you. You might love tap the most. It may be your *specialty,* and that's great, but a lack of ballet technique will diminish your working opportunities. Strive for more.

Broadening your technical skills means broadening your artistic and employment horizons. If you only sing pop style music, how can you be hired for a cruise ship requiring singers to perform in a pop show one night and then a Broadway revue and a bluesy jazz show the following nights? How can you expect to work for a repertory theater that runs a Shakespearean drama opposite a musical using the same cast if your skill set is entirely limited to one or the other? The performers who work the most are those who can cross over genres with ease. There are many ways you can apply the idea of versatility to your specific medium of study.

## ADVICE FOR ACTORS

The ability to embody a character takes a lot of skill. Different period styles and mediums require different skill sets. True theater training will give you a solid foundation to build from as an actor. Work on contemporary and classical pieces—the language and posture are very different. Learn the art of comedic timing. Take movement classes to learn period physicality and how to relate to an environment. Learn a technique for delivering precise dialects. Read new and classic screenplays and scripts often. Projecting on stage and minimizing for the camera require opposing techniques, but you should know how to do both. Train your voice to both speak and sing in healthy ways. Learn to play an instrument. Take yoga to better your agility and classes in history and psychology to better analyze a character. Study different acting techniques and use what works best for you. Stanislavsky, Strasburg, Meisner, Hagen—all can be valid techniques. Take courses in stage fighting and combat. Learn to improvise. Also, learn to dance both period social dances and styles for musical theater (or is it theatre?).[2]

---

[2] Theater vs. Theatre: Beyond the spelling, the difference is there is no difference. The word is not defined by the physical space versus the art form, but the origin of the spelling difference is interesting. You should look it up.

Emmy Award winner Jessica Walter has worked as an actress across just about every medium—ranging from stage plays to musicals, film, television, animation, commercials—you name it. Her well-respected work spans several decades and continues to be embraced by audiences. Jessica attributes her versatility to her early training.

> *I went to the Neighborhood Playhouse, a famous acting school in New York. Among my classmates were Christopher Lloyd, Dabney Coleman, Brenda Vaccaro, James Caan, and producer Jerry Weintraub. It was a really good class!! If you have the right training (basically if you start out with theatre as I did), I think that is the foundation to go into anything whether it's voiceover, animation, comedy, drama, or musicals (you have to be able to sing). I think everything comes from a basic truth. The process of the work is the same and it serves every single medium.*

## ADVICE FOR DANCERS

Every style of dance offers something unique, enhances other skills, and adds to what one offers artistically. A strong technical base in ballet, jazz, and modern is recommended across the board. Theater dance will give you stylistic training. Contemporary will heighten your connection to music and artistic interpretation. Hip-hop will give you strength, attack, and an ability to control isolations down to the intricate level. Tap will better your rhythm and musicality. Let go of your inhibitions—you *will* be asked to improvise in auditions, and if you can't sing it's time to find your voice! You cannot let fear keep you from developing necessary skills. Muscles, like your vocal cords, can be trained. Even commercial dancers may be asked to sing.

Go to acting class—it will help you communicate a better story and may lead to more opportunities within a job and higher pay. Learn to tumble even if it is just a couple tricks. All ladies *must* learn how to dance in heels. Whether it is Broadway, a tap show, a cruise ship, or a hip-hop video, it will be assumed that you know how to dance in heels. Start practicing now. Seriously. And, by the way, how is that ballet technique looking? Ballet combinations are still common "first cuts" at auditions.

Aerial and circus tricks are becoming more common throughout the entertainment industry. Joshua Dean, aerial choreographer, co-founder of 2 Ring Circus, and Pace University faculty member in New York City, recommends training in aerial/circus work (silks, lire, web, straps, etc.) in addition to dance.

> *Circus tricks are now often used in theatre, concert work, commercial dance, cruise ships, industrials, theme parks, and more. Several Broadway shows require some sort of aerial work. Dancers should definitely have aerial training. I have had so many students that pop into the school [Aerial Arts NYC] and say, "I have an audition this weekend and they want me to do silks. I took a couple silk classes three years ago. Can you get me ready?" It doesn't work that way. That's like taking tap dance for three years and then taking one ballet class before auditioning for ABT. That's delusional. This training is hard and it takes study.*

## ADVICE FOR SINGERS

Voices don't tend to fully mature until early adulthood, so keep working to build technique. Learn to be a soloist but also to hold your own harmony in a chorus or ensemble. Develop your belt, mix, and legit placements. Study classical to pop music and everything in between. They are all strongly related, but each requires a true stylist. Learn to act your song by taking acting classes and studying character development. Learn to dance—really dance—both classical and contemporary dance styles. You will be asked to execute specific choreography in auditions and stage shows most of the time. Dance training will increase your stamina, physical agility, and stage presence. Learn about music theory and how to actually read sheet music. When handed an original piece, this skill will allow you to contribute more as an artist as well as prepare for auditions and callbacks. Learn to play an instrument (or more than one). Strengthen your core and take yoga. Study with different teachers and coaches to get different perspectives and learn new techniques.

Amy Jo Slater has been a leading vocalist on multiple cruise line contracts that have taken her around the world and back. She has performed in a variety of revue style productions for Royal Caribbean, Renaissance, and Holland America cruise lines, each requiring different vocal skills.

> *As a featured vocalist on Royal Caribbean, I am required to have a solid grasp on several different musical styles. At any moment during a show, the style can*

*change from musical theatre to R&B to jazz. Vocally, expand your repertoire. I trained as a classical singer. I call classical technique "the ballet of the voice." You can use it to maintain healthy singing practices, give you longevity in your career, and aid you in singing though certain vocal issues (i.e., sickness or fatigue).*

Mark Hansen heads the musical theater program at the University of Wisconsin-Stevens Point and has musically directed for several San Francisco Bay Area theaters. He advises singers and actors to take their dance training seriously.

*Get your butts into dance classes now! There isn't an actor or singer on earth who hasn't benefitted from being able to move or having awareness of their bodies. Musicals demand dance from all parties these days, and the more you can do the more you will be in demand as a performer.*

# KEEP TRAINING THROUGHOUT YOUR CAREER

The training doesn't stop once the degree is in hand or your studio program has concluded. As artists, we can never stop improving. Keep going to dance classes to refine your skills and learn new styles. Keep taking audition and acting technique classes. Keep scheduling those private vocal sessions with a good industry coach. Continuing your education throughout your career not only allows for networking opportunities, it also provides the opportunity to build and maintain your skills, stay current, and keep up with the changes your body will go through as you continue to age. You can change or improve your trajectory well into your career as you train in new areas. A true artist has no finish line when it comes to becoming a better artist—we keep learning.

# Chapter Two

# Jobs and Markets

Congratulations on completing your degree, internship, or scholarship program! You should be proud of your accomplishment—it's a big step toward creating a successful career. Your major period of training is your jumping-off point into a new, very real kind of work. Careers are not things that suddenly happen to you—the work you pursue allows a career to develop over time. To know where to begin, it is important to understand what type of work is out there and where you can go to book those jobs. This chapter breaks down various performance opportunities and the major U.S. markets for professional performing artists.

## CATEGORIES OF PROFESSIONAL WORK

By simple definition, the label "professional" means you are paid by others to contribute your artistic services. We are fortunate that the U.S. has a wealth of opportunities for performing artists to be paid for their work. There are varying performance outlets, or "mediums", for professionals to work in cities across the country, and most performers find work in more than one genre across a career. If your training is diverse, you will find you are not limited to just working in one part of the field. Here you'll find a comprehensive breakdown of employment mediums for professional performers along with details such as union status, contract length and the common ranges of pay one might expect to receive.

---

# PAY SCALE RANGE

o   Low Range...............................$50-$500 per week
o   Middle Range.........................$500-$1,200 per week
o   High Range.................$1,200-$2,500 or more per week

Star Status Range: Though some go into show business with
dreams of fame and fortune, only a fractional percentage of
performers ever actually see fees in the millions. Even less will earn
those fees repeatedly over several years. Extreme wealth is an
unrealistic expectation.

---

- **Broadway:** In New York City, there are roughly 40 theaters that
  can call themselves a Broadway house and present live stage
  productions of plays and musicals, both new works and revivals.
  Performers work under a union "production contract," the highest
  paying contract under Actors' Equity Association's jurisdiction.
  (AEA is one of the unions for stage performers.) After a
  substantial rehearsal and preview[3] period, Broadway shows may run
  for a limited time or be open-ended, and generally are performed
  eight times per week. In a long-running show, as performers leave
  for various reasons, replacements are auditioned and put in. Pay is
  in the high range.

- **Burlesque/Cabaret:** Piano bars, lounges, comedy clubs,
  nightclubs, drag clubs, and cabaret venues offer opportunities for
  performers or specialty acts. These shows allow performers an
  artistic outlet to share their many varied talents. In large cities, it is

---

[3] Preview: A performance of a live show for a paying audience prior to the official opening
night. Previews allow the creative team and cast the opportunity to gauge how an audience
reacts and make changes to the show. Critics are generally not invited until the end of the
preview period or on opening night.

possible to make money from ticket sales or performance fees and gain an audience following. Pay is usually in the low range, and many performances are self-produced.

- **Casinos**: Gambling casinos in legal markets such as Las Vegas, Atlantic City, and Reno/Lake Tahoe or those on riverboats and Native American reservations often have showrooms or theaters that house live entertainment. Styles of shows vary but include: music or variety productions, magic or illusions, dance and pop music revues, headliner concerts, musicals, impersonators, topless/follies showgirls, specialty acts, and more. Shows usually perform six nights per week and sometimes two shows per night. Pay range can vary, though they generally pay in the middle to high range in bigger markets. Most shows are non-union, but employers might offer health benefits, housing, and meals through the hotel. Contract lengths are usually less than a year, but there are several open-ended shows running in Las Vegas and Atlantic City.

- **Children's Theater:** These are theatrical productions geared toward an audience of children that hire adult performers. Productions may target a specific age range and are union or non-union depending upon the producer. Musicals, plays, and revues make up the majority of the genre. There are resident theaters across the country dedicated to producing children's theater and also production companies that create tours for theaters, schools, and military bases/USO. Contract lengths vary, and pay ranges from the low to middle range.

- **Cirque-style Live Shows**: Inspired by the visionary style made popular by the Cirque du Soleil Company, these shows feature a variety of circus tricks and gymnastics as well as dance and live music. They require specialized performance skills. Productions have long-term runs in resident theaters and hotel/casinos or they tour. Pay can vary from low to middle range, but headlining acts can earn in the higher range. Contract lengths vary from three to six months and sometimes up to two years.

- **Commercials TV/Print**: Advertising campaigns use actors, dancers, models, voiceover artists, and more on television, the web, and in print. Shoots generally involve long hours over one or two days. Pay can vary depending on the union status and whether the campaign runs on national network, cable, or local television. Payment is through a buy-out[4] or a day rate, and you earn long-term residuals[5] on union contracts. If an actor's face or scenes are cut from the final version, a principal contract can be downgraded or out-graded affecting residual payments.

- **Concert Dance**: Many cities and towns across the country are home to independent choreographers and small companies offering performance opportunities for local dancers. Concerts, showings, and festivals are some of the venues where works are shown. The frequency of the performances is dependent on the ambitions and finances of the choreographer or company. Dancers receive little to no pay, but they can find artistic fulfillment as well as performance and networking opportunities.

- **Cruise Lines**: The cruising industry continues to grow and provide different entertainment for passengers each night. Most lines employ resident casts of singers and dancers onboard, and they book specialty acts, aerialists, ballroom couples, adagio couples, comedians, and illusionists in a variety of production shows, revues, cirque, solo acts, and musicals. Standard contracts are six months onboard plus a rehearsal period on land, but length can be shorter or longer depending on the producer or needs of the ship. Pay is usually in the middle range, but it can be on the high end for soloists on some lines. The lack of living expenses while working onboard is a great way for performers to save money and see the world. Shows are produced either by the cruise line itself or by an

---

[4] Buy-out: When a performer is paid a one-time fee without opportunity to earn further residuals. Usually applies to non-union film, television and commercials.
[5] Residual: An additional monetary payment to the performer if a filmed, taped, or recorded performance is aired more than once or is broadcast beyond the initially negotiated period of time, market, or media. See www.sagaftra.org FAQs for more information.

independent production company. Most companies hire performers from the U.S. and abroad. Contracts are non-union, but union members may work on ships due to the international status.

- **Dance Companies**: Professional dance companies specializing in various genres of dance for stage concerts are usually not-for-profit companies ranging in size. There are prestigious, well-paying, full-time companies in major cities; medium-sized companies in other markets that employ some full-time dancers or job in[6] guest artists; and small companies that pay dancers per performance. Some large U.S.-based companies—American Ballet Theatre, Alvin Ailey American Dance Theater, Hubbard Street Dance Chicago, San Francisco Ballet, Paul Taylor Dance Company for example—present resident seasons and major international touring and are world-renowned. Midsized companies present resident seasons with some regional, national, or international touring. Small companies perform works in regional dance festivals and present local seasons. Bigger companies offer union contracts (AGMA), health insurance, and retirement benefits. The pay scale varies according to the size, funding, and union status of the company as well as the number of performances and weeks employed per year. Some major companies have affiliated training schools to farm new and future company members. Auditions for jobs with major companies are fiercely competitive, and though positions do open up, dancers tend to stay with companies long term. There are hundreds of smaller companies that may not offer full-time employment but pay dancers per performance throughout a season.

- **Dinner Theater**: These are professional theaters presenting full-length musicals, revues, or plays where patrons get a full meal and a show all for one price. They present long-running productions or a season of shows. The pay scale is in the lower to middle range with

---

[6] Job in: When a performer is hired and brought in for one production or concert as opposed to being hired for an entire season.

contract lengths varying per theater. Some have union contracts, but a majority of dinner theaters are non-union. In some companies, the actors may also serve as wait staff—it's good to find that out before you audition.

- **Feature Films/Studio**: Full-length films produced by the major motion picture companies employ union actors (and sometimes singers and dancers) in leading, supporting, and background roles or as animation models and Foley artists.[7] Contract lengths last from one to two days up to several months depending on the size of the role. Shooting occurs on an indoor sound stage, on a backlot or on location.[8] Union minimums pay in the middle to mostly high range with future residuals paid. Background extras and stand-ins are generally uncredited and receive a minimal day rate in the low range. Some actors treat extra and stand-in work as a means to an end to earn money while others make full-time careers out of it and are able to join SAG-AFTRA (the union for film and TV performers). Dancers are no longer considered background after spending years fighting for a specific union contract.

- **Fringe Theater**: Plays or musicals produced with a low budget, usually new works but sometimes classics, are presented in theater or dance festivals as well as off-off-Broadway theaters and small theater/production companies. Performers donate their time or receive a low-range stipend fee. Union performers appear under a "showcase code" agreement that places limits on how much time can be asked of the actor. Money is not a reason to do a fringe show—it is a chance to be a part of a new work, acquire networking opportunities, be seen by potential employers or agents, and maybe be a part of a commercial run of a show as it develops further. Fringe shows have gone to Broadway with original cast members.

---

[7] Foley artist: Creating human-related sounds (voices, tap steps, etc.) to enhance film or video in post-production (after shooting has ended).
[8] On location: Any set for filming that does not take place on an indoor sound stage or studio backlot. May be local or in another city, state, or country.

- **Guest Artist**: Other live performance companies (symphony orchestras, chorales, bands) occasionally employ guest singers, actors, and dancers to appear in specific concerts and pieces. Contract lengths are generally short with fees ranging across the spectrum depending on size and budget.

- **Improv Troupes:** These are regional companies devoted to the art of improvisational comedy. Performed in cabaret or theatrical settings, company members are given a variety of structured scenarios around which they improvise scenes and characters in front of a live audience. Audience participation is usual. Pay can be low to middle range, and actors have been known to segue into solo stand-up or film/TV/stage jobs after training and performing in an improv troupe. Improvisational comedy is closely tied to TV sketch comedy.

- **Independent/Short Films**: These films, either full-length or short, are usually not produced by a major motion picture company, though, if successful, they are picked up for distribution by one of those companies. Pay rates are usually at low union minimums, as budgets tend to be limited, but there are still residual opportunities. Lengths of the shoot and locations vary. Films are sometimes entered into film festivals and make money off DVD/download sales/TV broadcasts resulting in residual payments.

- **Industrials**: Live shows or short films are sometimes associated with a specific product, company, or industry. These are different than television commercials or print ads. Examples include: performing to introduce a new product at a trade show, performing for a private event or party, acting in an instructional training video, television infomercials, entertaining or a meet-and-greet[9] at a company convention, sponsored/paid flash mobs, etc. Usually, live industrials have minimal rehearsal and are only performed one

---

[9] Meet-and-greet: When performers meet and interact with audience members or patrons in person before or after a performance.

time, meaning performers only have one chance to "get it right." Pressure on performers is high. Industrials pay across all ranges depending on the size and budget.

- **Magic/Illusionist Shows:** The art of stage magic has been intriguing audiences for years. Magicians must study and practice their craft as much as any other type of performing artist. Specializing in sleight of hand and/or prop-based illusions, they must be good actors and possess creativity and stage presence. Magicians often incorporate magic assistants, dancers, prop technicians, and sometimes singers into their productions. Pay can range from the low to middle ranges depending upon the venue and producer.

- **Music Concert Tours:** Best-selling recording artists and music labels produce concert tours each year. They mostly play one to two nights in a venue with bookings across the country and sometimes the world. Many hire other performers—dancers, backup singers, and specialty acts—to perform in the show alongside the headliner. These jobs may also lead to additional performance opportunities with that particular artist or group. Contracts range from a few months to a couple of years and pay in the higher range for artists backed by a major record label.

- **Music Videos:** The Internet changed the music video industry (short films using a popular song/artist) in terms of budgets and level of profile, but there is still opportunity. Utilizing commercial dancers, models, and actors, these shoots can last anywhere from a couple of days to a couple of weeks, sometimes with additional rehearsal days. Pay rates for music videos aren't great (minimal day rate and no residuals) when video contracts are non-union buyouts[10]; however, this is something union performers are working hard to change.

---

[10] Non-union buyout: A contract for a film, commercial, video, or reality television show where performers are paid a flat fee and are not eligible for any additional payment or residuals no matter how long the material is used or shown in public.

- **National Tours/Broadway**: If a show, musical or play, finds success on Broadway, producers will send the production out on tour to major markets around the country. A production might sit down in a big city like Chicago, Los Angeles, San Francisco, or Toronto for an extended period of time, and/or travel from city to city playing anywhere from three or four days (split-week tours), one or two weeks, or one to three-month engagements in each stop. There are times when a show is sent on the road "pre-Broadway" with the hopes it will end up playing in New York after gaining popularity and capital. National tours audition and rehearse in a point-of-origin city, do tech in an interim city, and open in the first scheduled city. Contracts are generally six months long, but they may become open-ended depending upon the length of the tour and nature of the principal or chorus contract. Performers receive a salary and per diem.[11] These union tours can pay the same high range rate as Broadway contracts or be tiered to different minimums across the full range of pay.

- **National Tours/Non-Union**: Tours of musicals and plays that employ non-union talent are more affordable for producers and presenters in large part because salaries, benefit payment, and per diems take out a much smaller chunk of production costs. Non-union tours are created for one of three reasons: the show is being scaled down after completing a union tour to play smaller markets; the producer has chosen to bypass a first national union tour altogether (thus giving up the ability to employ headlining Broadway talent); or the producer has decided to mount a new production without recent Broadway ties. Traveling on a bus, stops may involve a one-night performance (the infamous "one-nighter") or sit-downs up to a couple weeks. Non-union tours mostly employ young professionals, providing them ways to cut their teeth

---

[11] Per diem: A pre-negotiated amount of money paid weekly to the performer, in addition to the salary, used to pay for living expenses on the road. Is generally non-taxed. Performers use it to cover hotel, food, and local expenses.

and work with Broadway creative teams.[12] Contract lengths vary depending upon the total weeks the tour is booked, though some non-union tours have open-ended runs. Pay is generally in the low to middle ranges.

- **National Tours/Children's Shows**: These tours are live-action stage versions of popular children's television shows or films, such as *Sesame Street* or Disney Channel and Nickelodeon series. Performers dance in "character" costumes with large puppet-like heads or play "face characters" (which means you must physically resemble the original cartoon or actor). Shows are sung live or lip-synced to a track. These tours play large arenas, stadiums, and theaters, usually one or two nights in each city, and performers mainly travel on a bus. Contract lengths vary and are mostly non-union with some exceptions. Pay scales tend to be in the middle range and include salary and per diem.

- **National Tours/Commercial Dance**: These tours play nightclubs, theaters, casinos, arenas, or concert venues. Generally, the show is themed and may showcase a specific type of dance (Irish step dancing, ballroom, etc.) or is crafted around the music catalogue of a particular artist or visual idea. Live singers or character actors may also be a part of these productions. Pay range and contract length will vary.

- **Off-Broadway**: These are theatrical productions in New York City that are not in a Broadway theater but in one of about 50 official off-Broadway theaters with a seating capacity of 100 to 499 (Broadway minimum is 500 seats). Both not-for-profit and commercial production companies produce off-Broadway. Shows include plays, musicals, revues, and other genres. Runs might be open ended, limited time, or a part of a season. Sometimes shows

---

[12] Creative team: The people behind the table responsible for the artistic creation of the show. This includes the director, choreographer, musical director/conductor, designers, and their associates/assistants as well as the writer, composer, and lyricist.

transfer from off-Broadway to Broadway (or vice versa), and they are usually union contracts. Range of pay depends on the size of the house, but salaries are generally in the middle range.

- **Opera**: The U.S. is home to large and small professional opera companies. They each have a resident chorus and hire guest artists for principal roles and dancers and supers[13] as needed. Companies under a union agreement (AGMA) pay a fee per performance (plus a per diem for performers from out of town) at union-negotiated minimums. Non-union companies usually follow the same payment structure, though the fees may be less. Operas use a full rehearsal period, with a limited number of performances that are spaced apart in order to allow for voices to rest. Fees are generally in the middle to high range for the large companies.

- **Pro Dance Teams**: NFL and NBA teams use professional dancers to provide halftime entertainment and possibly function as cheerleaders. Most weeks, dancers learn and perform new routines and travel on occasion. Dance team members also serve as club liaisons within the community and must commit to an entire season full of weekly rehearsals, travel, promotional events, and performances. Most teams do not pay their dancers a salary, though the performers receive a small stipend per game and other gifts and perks in lieu of a weekly salary.

- **Radio City Christmas Spectacular**: It's hard to put Radio City into a specific category, so it has its own! This seasonal production runs at Radio City Music Hall in New York with additional sit-down or touring companies in other cities. More than a hundred performers are hired as lead characters, singers, ensemble dancers, or the World Famous Rockettes for this large-scale musical revue each season. After a month-long rehearsal period, the cast performs several shows *per day* throughout the holiday season.

---

[13] Super: Short for "supernumerary." A non-speaking, non-singing, non-dancing part in an opera or ballet. Usually supers are hired to make crowd scenes feel more full or to serve as extras.

Some years include a spring show as well. Performers work under a union contract (AGVA) and receive a weekly salary in the higher pay range. Dancers cast as Rockettes receive additional contractual perks throughout the year; some continue their employment year-round in a promotional capacity.

- **Readings/Workshops**: Part of the process of writing new work for theater or film involves asking performers to come together and read the script aloud to hear how the dialogue/music sounds and characters develop. Readings, staged readings, labs, and workshops—when all or part of the show starts to get put on its feet—are important parts of moving a new show forward and attracting potential producers or investors. Usually actors are not paid much for their work, if at all, but can potentially advance with the show and create new working relationships with directors. If working under an official union workshop contract, performers have a share in royalties if the show goes on to make money commercially even if that actor isn't asked to remain with the show.

- **Regional Theater**: Legitimate professional theaters operate across America from big cities to small towns. They present seasons of live musicals, revues, and plays. A run of one particular show might last a week or two to a few months. Union theaters belong to a variety of collective bargaining agreements with the actors' union. The type of contract dictates the pay minimums for each theater, though they run from the low end to upper middle range. One example is the LORT contract. LORT theaters belong to the League of Regional Theaters and are tiered A, B, C, or D depending on the size and budget of the company. (Visit www.actorsequity.org for details on regional contracts and theaters.) Most union theaters hire a blend of union and non-union performers—some hire non-union interns for an entire season. There are fully non-union regional theaters as well that don't pay as much as larger union companies, but many do quality work. Some non-union theaters hire leading union performers on guest artist contracts.

- **Resort Area Entertainment**: Tourism-heavy, non-gambling cities—such as Branson, Myrtle Beach, Pigeon Forge, Miami, and Orlando, to name a few—are known for their entertainment offerings. Hotels, resorts, or independent theaters present production shows, magic shows, dinner theater, concerts, musicals, plays, and revues. Long-running shows usually offer six-month to one-year contracts. Other limited-time runs might be seasonal. Pay is usually in the middle range.

- **Student Films**: Both graduate and undergraduate film school students love to employ professional actors in film projects. These are nonpaying (you will see the words "Copy and Credit"[14] in the audition notices) but can offer great on-camera experience, free footage for use on your demo reel and promotional website, and the opportunity for occasional entry into film festivals. Today's film students are tomorrow's major directors, so it isn't a bad way to network and set oneself up for future prospects and career longevity.

- **Summer Stock**: Seasonal theaters that operate primarily in the summer months might do just one stage production, run multiple shows in rep[15], or present a new show every week or two (meaning you perform one show at night while learning the next one during the day). Rehearsals are short periods of only one or two weeks. Companies may be union, with contracts collectively bargained like regional theaters, or non-union. Pay is usually on the lower end of the scale, though some large union theaters pay in the upper middle range.

- **Television/Scripted Series**: In addition to hiring series regular actors in leading roles, long-running series hire actors for guest star,

---

[14] Copy and credit: Instead of receiving a fee, the producer agrees to list your name in the film credits and promotional material and send you a final copy of the film for your own promotional use.

[15] Shows in rep: This refers to repertory theater, a theater that presents two or more shows at the same time rotating them every other night in the same space, at times with the same actors. Many times this happens in summer stock or festival situations.

recurring, day player, or under five[16] roles throughout a season. Pilots are created each season to test out and sell new show ideas to networks and viewers. Actors are hired per episode unless they are a series regular—someone who contractually appears on all or most episodes in a season. The hiring of dancers and singers for specific episodes depends upon the storyline or concept. Union actors are paid a day rate (hours can be long) or fee per episode and make residuals each time the episode is rebroadcast, sold into syndication, downloaded, or sold as a DVD. The potential to make money on the higher end of the pay scale is great. Genres include sitcoms and dramas as well as reenactments, soap operas, movies, miniseries, variety shows, and more. Background extras and stand-ins, just as in film, receive a low-range day rate but no residuals. The shooting of one episode can last from one to 14 days.

- **Television/Reality Shows:** This genre of television as it relates to professional performers includes talent competitions, hosting, industry-themed shows, game shows, talk shows, major awards ceremonies, or any shows about people of interest. On-camera talent contracted to appear in reality shows make a fee per episode. Whether or not residuals are paid is hit or miss, as most reality shows are non-union. Depending on the show or network, fees paid can be anywhere in the low range up to the high range. Reality shoots don't tend to require much rehearsal time, unless it is a competition show, and schedules will vary.

- **Theme Parks:** Disney, Universal, and Six Flags are some of the biggest names in year-round park entertainment. There are many regional parks that are seasonal across the country as well. Most theme parks present live entertainment featuring actors, singers, and dancers in concert, comedy, character or musical revues, parades, and meet-and-greets. Performers perform multiple shows

---

[16] Guest star: a substantial role in one episode of a series; Recurring: a character who appears in several episodes; Day player: an actor hired for one day of shooting; Under five: A small role where the actor speaks only five lines or fewer.

per day and may do some costume or face character work. Year-round parks offer longer contracts, while seasonal parks only offer contracts for the summer months. Some offer union contracts. Pay can be in the low range but is usually in the middle range.

- **Voiceovers**: Commercials, animation, public service announcements, and TV/film/radio shows employ the services of trained voiceover actors. Some contracts are union and can earn residuals. Pay scale can mirror that of commercials, television, and film and is usually in the middle to high end. Contract lengths will vary per project but are usually short.

- **Web Series**: The industry of creating series shown only on the Internet is evolving. As advertisers, subscription services, and unions get more involved, performers are seeing greater opportunities for paying work. But industry standards are still undefined, so participating in a web series is non-paying a majority of the time. SAG-AFTRA, the film/television union, has negotiated a standard contract for the participation of its members. Though the standard contract does not determine a fee, it does protect the actors from abuse, and there is a residual structure in place should a series be sold on DVD or download. Schedules will vary and shooting days may not be consecutive as most series are independently produced. The web series industry is changing more rapidly than any other and will soon be a more viable source of income for more performers.

- **International Work for Americans**: Some U.S.-based production companies hire American performers for shows they produce overseas, such as USO tours of military bases, musical theater tours, or resident production shows. Also, some foreign producers seek to hire Americans for touring musicals, resident production shows, theme parks, cruise ships, and major dance and opera companies in other countries. Many American performers find themselves working in Canada, Japan, China, the United Kingdom, France, South Korea, The Netherlands, Italy, Greece, Germany, Australia, Argentina, and Mexico, as well as various Caribbean island nations. The pay range depends upon the type of job and the producer. Beware when negotiating—there are instances when American performers are presented with a "new" contract upon arriving in another country that differs greatly from the initial contract that was signed.

# MAJOR U.S. MARKETS FOR PROFESSIONALS

Life for the professional performer would be simpler if every community in America offered us full-time employment options. Our reality: a career as a performer means a life of travel and/or relocation. We are "the gypsies." There are smaller communities where professional work is available at sporadic times throughout the year, but a majority of career-oriented performers end up in a larger market simply because they offer the most audition opportunities. Producers from across the country hold auditions in these markets to access the larger talent pools. The largest markets—New York City, Los Angeles, Chicago, Las Vegas, Orlando—offer the most opportunities to work as a performer full-time. Other major U.S. cities provide plenty of opportunities for performers to make a living and enjoy a different quality of life. Every city has something different to offer you as a performer, and it is important to find the city that appeals to your dreams and talents.

## NEW YORK CITY

"The Big Apple"—the American birthplace for theater, film, television, and major performing arts companies for well over 100 years—remains an international hub for the arts. New professionals move here every day for training and for work. Many performers come to New York with dreams of singing and dancing on Broadway, but with thousands and thousands of performing artists living in the city, not everyone can be in a Broadway show at the same time! Thankfully, the industry for performing artists is vast and diverse opportunities abound.

In addition to Broadway, there's also off-Broadway theater featuring plays, musicals, song cycles, and revues. MSG produces the *Radio City Music Hall Christmas Spectacular* here every season, and auditions are held in New York for the double-cast resident NYC production as well as regional and touring productions of the show. Some seasons they produce a spring show as well. The cabaret and burlesque performance scenes are huge. The Manhattan Association of Cabarets and Clubs (MAC) Awards and Bistro Awards are given to exceptional cabaret performers each season, and the city is a major stop on the international burlesque circuit. Readings, workshops, and showcases of new work happen often.

New York is the second-largest market in the U.S. for the film and television industry after Los Angeles. There are several network, cable, and Internet series shot here in residence and New York is a physical backdrop for many feature and independent films each year. A large number of advertising and marketing firms call New York home, so the industry for performing in commercials on television, radio, and the web is big. Live and filmed industrials are cast and rehearsed in New York to be performed here or elsewhere.

Major opera companies, including the New York-based Metropolitan Opera and others from around the world, audition singers and also find dancers here. Chorales and guest artist contracts with symphonies provide additional work opportunities for classically trained singers based in the city.

New York is home to a multitude of dance companies—from internationally recognized to regionally touring to small "rehearse in a warehouse" in size—and concert dance thrives in the "downtown" scene. Some large dance companies have affiliated schools. Opportunities for commercial and hip-hop dancers include network and cable television, music videos, feature and independent film, awards shows, TV commercials, stage tours, and more, though the overall commercial dance scene is smaller than it is in Los Angeles.

Even if the work itself may not take place in New York, many producers hold auditions here to access the large talent pool. Both union and non-union national tours audition performers and hold rehearsals here before traveling the country. Some European, Chinese and other international tours seek American talent in New York as well. You will also find both union and non-union auditions for cruise lines, casino

productions, theme parks, and most professional regional, di⸱
summer stock theaters from the tri-state area and across the

## LOS ANGELES

The "City of Angels" grew into what it is today because the film
industry adopted it as its home early in the 20th century. There are those
performers who move to Hollywood with the hope of achieving stardom
by being randomly discovered working at a coffee shop (or at a party, or
shopping at the mall, etc.) by a "big director." Has that happened? Sure. Do
I personally know someone who had it happen somewhat this way? Yes,
actually. Are the odds in your favor? No. No, they are not. If that is your
plan for discovery, it's a bad plan. Finding work in L.A. requires the
performer to navigate the business in a more productive way than just
waiting around to be "discovered."

Los Angeles is the largest market in the world for film and television
across all genres, and much of the L.A. economy relies on the industry and
the support it requires. All of the major motion picture and television
studios are based here and film in soundstages, on studio lots, and on
location throughout the city. Even films and TV shows that shoot
elsewhere hold auditions to cast L.A.-based actors. The city is also home to
smaller independent production companies that create films, television
series and specials that are sold to or distributed by the larger film and
network studios. The high-end resources that are available to create quality
advertising campaigns make L.A. a busy market for commercial and
voiceover actors and models. There is also industrial work, both on film
and live on stage, created and produced in L.A.

For commercial dancers, L.A. is *the* place—from world concert tours
to music videos, club shows to movie musicals, awards shows to TV
commercials and more, there is not a bigger market for commercial dance
in America. Tours and resident stage productions bound for other markets
will many times originate and rehearse in L.A. The burlesque scene provides
opportunities for dancers and specialty acts. For concert dancers, you'll find
many small and medium-sized dance companies based here.

Backup singers who perform commercially with pop stars can find
work in concert tours, promotional appearances, music videos and other

formances. The cabaret scene for singers has remained healthy. Several production companies that produce entertainment for cruise ships are based in the L.A. area. They hold auditions for singers and dancers and also rehearse at their in-house local studios. Southern California (including Orange County) is home to theme parks with live shows (Disneyland, Universal Studios, Knott's Berry Farm, etc.) that operate year-round.

Los Angeles is also has its share of resident opera and theater companies—both large and small. L.A. Opera and the Center Theatre Group are the resident companies downtown at the Los Angeles Music Center and small companies reside across the area. Though L.A. is an A-list stop for Broadway national tours, there are highly successful Broadway shows known to send resident sit-down companies to L.A. They may stay several years and cast local performers. There are also Broadway shows that have originated in Southern California (L.A. or San Diego) before transferring to New York. The regional theater scene within the L.A. area has grown smaller in the past decade, but many opportunities still exist for union and non-union performers. Outside regional and summer stock theaters from across the western United States also hold auditions in L.A. There are also workshops and readings of new works.

## CHICAGO

The largest market between the coasts, the "Windy City" is central to the professional performing arts scene in the Midwest. Many professionals build entire careers in Chicago with much success. Because the scene is a bit smaller, others find Chicago to be a great stepping-stone market. They either begin a career here prior to moving to New York or L.A., or relocate here after spending years in one of those larger markets.

Chicago has a healthy local theater scene with opportunities for both union and non-union performers to work in musicals and plays. The League of Chicago Theatres lists more than 200 theater companies in the area—some theater companies send shows directly to Broadway often with a Chicago-based cast. As they have for decades, Broadway shows play out-of-town tryouts or install resident sit-down companies in Chicago and often hold local auditions in both instances.

Though it is smaller, there is a thriving market for work in television series, feature and independent film, and commercials. Chicago is home to many renowned professional concert dance companies, opera companies, and improvisational comedy troupes. Cruise lines, theme parks, and other live stage shows take advantage of the sizable talent pool at Chicago auditions, as do regional and summer stock theaters from around the Midwest.

## LAS VEGAS

The professional scene in "Sin City" revolves around the hotel/casino industry, with many hotels housing one or more resident productions. These productions feature singers, dancers, and specialty acts in cirque shows, magic shows, follies-style showgirl revues, various themed revues, concerts with major headliners, or shortened versions of popular Broadway musicals. There are some revues that involve adult themes and ask some dancers (female and male) to perform topless. In Las Vegas and in general, always make sure you understand what you are auditioning for especially in regards to wardrobe. Being too strict about what you are willing to wear or not wear on stage in Vegas will limit the performing opportunities available to you.

The large nightclub scene employs professional go-go dancers and burlesque performers to perform in choreographed and individual sets. It is not uncommon for dancers in the hotel shows to also have additional gigs as go-go dancers a few nights a week. Some casinos employ actors in atmospheric performances playing characters related to the theme of the hotel. Las Vegas also has a large convention and trade show industry, with opportunities for industrial work. There is television, commercial, and film work for actors and specialty performers though the scene is not huge. Production companies that produce live entertainment for cruise lines, theme parks, resort areas, outside casino markets, and overseas venues hold annual auditions here to access the large talent pool. Some of these companies are based in Las Vegas as they also produce shows locally in the hotels.

Though some musicals and revues are union, a majority of shows have non-union status. Many times performers are provided health insurance, benefits, and meals through the hotel they are performing at.

## ORLANDO

Orlando is home to the largest theme parks in the country (Walt Disney World, Universal Studios, SeaWorld, Busch Gardens Tampa, and more) with several shows that provide year-round employment (with benefits) for singers, dancers, comedy/improv actors, stunt performers, aerialists, and costume character performers. Some are union contracts. There is a large convention and tradeshow industry with live industrial work, and also some resort area resident theaters housing cirque, musical revue, and stunt shows. Orlando has a small market for film, television, commercials, and regional theater.

At the center of the State of Florida, Orlando is not far from the several union and non-union regional and dinner theaters, cruise line entertainment producers, and industrial production companies across the region. Producers from outside the market (cruise ships, international theme parks, resort entertainment, commercial dance) hold auditions in Orlando to access the sizeable, young talent pool.

## SMALLER U.S. MARKETS

Additional cities that offer frequent work opportunities for professionals include:

- **San Francisco Bay Area, Seattle, Minneapolis/St. Paul, Dallas/Ft. Worth, Washington D.C., Salt Lake City, Boston,** and **Philadelphia** all have multiple professional resident theater companies as well as opera companies and concert dance scenes. There is also film and TV production on the local and national levels.

- **Branson, Atlantic City, Pigeon Forge,** and **Myrtle Beach** are tourist heavy resort towns with long-running production shows, theme parks, theaters, and/or casinos that hire singers, dancers, actors, and specialty acts for seasonal and full-time work.

- **Atlanta, Miami/Ft. Lauderdale, New Orleans,** and **Albuquerque** are popular filming locations for the feature film industry, and entire television series are shot in or near these cities. Atlanta also has a thriving hip-hop scene for both dance and music.

- **Nashville** and **Houston** are communities where singers (country, pop and classical/opera) can make a living and study. Both cities feature professional theater and dance companies as well as some film and TV production.

Of course, these are not the only cities across the country where professional work can be found—do your research to find the opportunities that exist in any given city. Keep in mind that smaller markets do not exclusively hire local performers for the big jobs. It is common for companies in smaller markets to hold auditions in bigger cities to access larger talent pools. They frequently job talent in.

Some people decide to stay in their hometowns with the intent of "flying out" to major cities for auditions. They also audition online and through video submissions. This strategy has been successful for some, but will most definitely prove difficult and costly. Flying is expensive, a majority of the industry does not cast exclusively online (yet…), and attending those last-minute crucial callbacks isn't necessarily possible. The probability is not high that you will achieve a full-time career as a performer this way, but some people make that sacrifice in order to stay near family, maintain a certain quality of life, or for personal reasons. You decide what the right location is for you. So much of landing work means being in the "right place"—you just have to make sure you are in the right place at the right time.

# DECIDING WHERE TO GO

If you aren't quite ready to commit to moving to a large market, perhaps a smaller city is a good place for you to gain professional experience and training first. Some performers choose to stay in a small market and build lives without ever moving to New York or L.A.; others use smaller markets as a steppingstone before moving on to a large market; and some move to New York or L.A. the day after graduation. In this business, everyone has to follow his or her own path. After college, I lived and worked in Orlando for a couple of years earning my Equity card and saving money before moving to New York. That worked out well for me. My other college classmates moved straight to New York after graduation and began working and auditioning. That worked out well for them. Everyone is different. There is no exclusive formula. You have to make the choices that appeal to you.

Jump in the pool! You can't make a wrong choice in deciding where to move as long as you make a choice and commit to the market you are in. If a certain type of work is interesting to you or you get a great job offer, go where that work is. Moving to New York or L.A. is not a requirement in order to have a successful career—hundreds of thousands of professionals have proven that to be true over time. But being in the right place at the right time means you need to be where auditions are happening.

## PREPARING FOR THE MOVE

I know more than a few people who moved to L.A. or New York with $100 in their pocket and a dream. They found cheap apartments in scary neighborhoods, pounded the pavement for a day job, and began auditioning for anything they could. There's nothing to say you can't do it that way. I decided early on that approach wasn't for me.... As you decide for yourself, and for your own mental health, consider these suggestions when strategizing your move:

- ✓ **Go experience the city.** If you have never been to the major market that interests you, plan an extended visit before deciding to make the full move—see the sights, take some drop-in classes, meet up with friends in the industry there, see some shows, and maybe go to an audition. Plan to spend anywhere from a week to a month in order to experience the environment. You will quickly discover whether or not the city feels like the right fit.

- ✓ **Save your pennies**. How much money in the bank is enough? Your personal decision should factor in the variables. It may take you some time to find regular sources of income in a new city, but

regardless, you will need to start paying rent ($600 to $1,200 or
more per month in the larger markets—not cheap) and you might
want to eat something right from the start. Factor in more for
utilities and transportation. Will you need a car? (New York, no.
L.A., yes. Chicago, maybe.) Make an expense list of what you
project you would need to live on for the first two to three months
as a start. Keep in mind that signing a lease on an apartment  → 3 mos
requires first month's rent and a security deposit worth a second  rent
month's rent—and a third month's rent to cover the broker's fee in
New York—as well as a potential co-signer with proof of a steady
income.

✓ **Downsize your life**. If it doesn't fit into a couple suitcases and a
couple boxes, you probably don't need it—at least not right away.
Look into the possibility of subletting an apartment when you first
move. (That will save you paying a broker's fee but will still require
first month's rent and a deposit to start.) Finding an apartment to
sublet isn't that difficult in the major markets—performers are
constantly on the road[17] and looking for someone to cover their
rent and bills while away. Stay in contact with people you know in
the business for leads on housing—word of mouth is still the best
resource. There are also groups on Facebook and postings at union
offices where you can find sublets and shares. Living with people
who already know the ins and outs of the local market and
geography might prove to be helpful.

✓ **Strategize the timing**. Don't wait to do your market research until
you get there. Learn about the industry trends before you go so you
know if you are arriving just before, during, or after a big audition
season for that city. In Los Angeles, "pilot season" is a time when
several auditions are happening for new television series, usually
late January through early March. Episodic season begins in July
when established TV shows are coming back from hiatus to film

---

[17] On the road: Working at jobs that are away from your home city. May refer to actually
being on a tour, but also applies to regional or on-location gigs.

for the fall. In New York, the busiest time for musical theater auditions is February through April when summer stock and fall tours are being cast. Broadway shows for the following season will cast in late spring/early summer for an autumn opening, or late summer/early autumn for a spring opening. Chicago is the busiest in the spring for both theater and television auditions. Knowing what kinds of auditions to be prepared for up front is an important way to stay ahead of the game.

# PERFORMING ARTISTS FROM OUTSIDE OF THE U.S.

From a business perspective, this book is not about the ways the industry operates in other countries, but if you are a non-U.S. citizen reading this, you might have an interest in coming to the U.S. to pursue your dreams. People like you do this successfully all the time, but the factors that allow someone to work here will vary depending on where the person is coming from and the talents they have.

U.S. Immigration Laws change every so often. Work visas you can apply for vary (immigrant and non-immigrant), and some are more limiting than others in terms of the jobs you can accept. Most visas carry expiration dates and require you to go through a costly renewal process. Obtaining a "green card" allows you to work without restriction and follow a path to U.S. citizenship. If you are from another country and want to relocate here, you should acquire the services of a U.S. immigration lawyer who specializes in assisting performing artists through the legal process. It is expensive (several thousands of dollars), but it is the system we have—there are not viable ways to get around it.

Because immigration law is a federal practice, as opposed to a state law, your attorney can be based anywhere as long as they are licensed. It's possible to find cheaper fees in different parts of the country. Alex Isbell, Esq., is an attorney with Solow, Isbell & Palladino, LLC (Boston and

Philadelphia) who specializes in U.S. immigration law. He has helped artists with a desire to work in the United States. Below is Alex's advice for the two work visa approaches you should consider.

- **Immigrant Visa (Green Card) Options**
  - Family-Based Immigration Visas: *It's much faster and much cheaper, and it is the first place I turn in consultations to figure out how to counsel clients. In terms of using a family-based petition as a vehicle for a green card, we are probably only really talking about spousal petitions, parent to child (child means someone who is not married and under 21), and potentially child to parent petitions. One major caution: Don't marry someone just for papers. This leads to serious problems. The alien involved in the process could essentially be banned from the United States for life, and the U.S. citizen or permanent resident involved could face fines or jail time.*

  - Employment-Based Immigration Visas: *These are likely only going to be available for very established performers coming to the United States, because to qualify for this type of visa you have to demonstrate "extraordinary ability." Some real pros about this process are the facts that you can self-petition (i.e., you don't need a contract or job offer in the United States), the visas are always immediately available, and you can apply for the visa from anywhere in the world.*

- **Non-Immigrant Visa Options**
  *The main distinction between non-immigrant and immigrant visas/statuses is that a non-immigrant makes an implicit promise to return home at the end of his/her status in the U.S., whereas an immigrant is implicitly declaring that he/she wants to permanently live and work in the U.S. There are currently non-immigrant visas with designations from A through V. One example is:*

  - H-1B Visa: *This is the standard bread and butter employment-based visa in the United States. It has a few basic requirements: 1) a job offer from a U.S. employer, 2) for a job that requires a specific college degree as defined by the Department of Labor, 3) the person has to have that degree, and 4) the employer has to agree to pay at least the prevailing wage as set by the Department of Labor for the person's work in the U.S. These are valid for a maximum of six years and can be issued for a maximum of three years at a time.*

If you come over on a tourist or student visa with the intent to just stay and attempt to work professionally, you will find yourself mostly unemployed and extremely frustrated. Professional jobs are competitive, involve legal paperwork and contracts, and do not pay under the table. Coming to the U.S. legally is your only real option to freely participate in the business and work in order to make a living.

There is some strategy to getting ahead in the immigration process. The first thing you can do is to build up your resume by booking the jobs available in your home country. Keep good documentation of your work (programs, newspaper reviews, etc.). If you are landing the big jobs where you live and can prove you are exceptional, it can help your lawyer make your case. Train with the best schools you can. Work with any U.S.-based creative teams that might be visiting or teaching in your country to build connections. If in the U.S. on a student visa, make sure to study here with directors, choreographers, vocal coaches and other people whom you would hope to work with professionally. If they like you and want to hire you for a job, they may be willing to write a letter of recommendation for your portfolio or offer you a job with a sponsored work visa. Some performers visit the U.S. and land an agent here with connections to attorneys experienced in helping performers make the transition.

The immigration process and timeline will be different for everyone. There are never any guarantees, but if performing in the United States is your dream, it is possible it can happen for you.

# Chapter Three

# YOU ARE A SMALL BUSINESS. THINK LIKE A SMALL BUSINESS.

Successfully working in show business takes much more than just being a talented performer. Over the years, I have seen many talented, well-trained young performers attempt to pursue a professional career only to decide to change course after a *very* short time. It isn't an easy business—signing up to pursue your dreams also means signing up for a lot of rejection, sacrifice, fierce competition, a lack of stability, and decisions by higher-ups that seem unfair. That's the unfortunate reality. In general, the decision to leave the profession early seems to be less about falling out of love with the art form and more about being frustrated with the business in general. This book is here to help you avoid some of that frustration. Finding success in show business requires understanding the business—you can learn! Think of your career this way:

**You are your own small business.**

Performing artists are freelancers for the most part. We can work several different jobs in a year, our tax forms consist of W-2s from certain employers, 1099s from jobs where we are independent contractors, per diems, receipts for the expenses we can legally write off, and payments to various contract laborers (agents, unions, coaches, etc.). The government basically considers you a small business, where you are the sole proprietor. Successful small business owners understand these six important factors: product, market analysis, skill maintenance, networking, marketing, and strategy. All of them apply to you as a performing artist.

# PRODUCT

Every small business exists to sell a product its owner hopes others will buy. In this case, you and your talent are the product. Small businesses become successful when customers can identify their brand. In this business, you yourself become a brand. You are selling your brand to every producer, director, choreographer, and casting director for whom you audition. Your professional name is the name of your business and identifies your brand. People will begin to associate your name with the talent you bring to the table. The goal is for your name to carry a reputation—hopefully a good one!

## PROFESSIONAL NAME

Statistically, most performers do not change from their given names. Some may add their middle name or initial in order to distinguish themselves from another performer, but it is important that you have a name you can professionally identify with. Be proud of your name. Gus Kaikkonen, a director of several off-Broadway plays who first enjoyed success as a Broadway actor, suggests that you consider early on what bearing your birth name might have on your career.

> *Change your name if you need to so that it fits your product, meaning your own look and where you want to take your career. Archie Leach may have had a career, but he never would have become Cary Grant.*

Gus has accomplished an enviable career with his colorful last name of Finnish origin, but his advice is worth considering. If changing your name is something you feel you need to do, it is a decision you need to make early on. There are people who go by one name professionally even though they legally go by something else. Their professional name is the name of their business (just make sure your employer writes the check to the name matching your actual bank account if you do that…).

Some performers are required to alter their name upon joining one of the unions, as no two people are allowed to use the exact same name within a union's living roster. There is also the issue of changing your last name should you get married. Some people change it; some don't. Some people hyphenate both names. The decision to change to a married name depends on how branded you have become. Changing later in a career may impact how professional colleagues find you or recognize your work. If you are brand new to the business and just got married, changing your name probably isn't a big deal—you are still establishing your reputation.

## TYPE

You and your talent are the product being sold—to understand that product you must "know yourself." You can do this by identifying your "type." We are all born with our own distinct features, shades, and fingerprints. As kids, we learn that we are each unique—there is no one else on Earth just like you! Reality check—the commercial entertainment business doesn't always see it that way. It is a world of boxes. Generally, when a performer walks into an audition room, he or she is immediately assessed by variables consisting of height, weight, gender, ethnicity, features, bone structure, size measurements, vocal range, special skills, technical ability, what existing star/actor/dancer/singer they look or sound like, and other factors. All of these factors add up to what your type is.

When writers or directors are envisioning a new piece, many times they have an idea of the types of performers they believe are suited to specific roles. "Typecasting" is a tool casting directors use to narrow down candidates to the specifications of the overall vision for a production. Perhaps the storyline calls for actors of a certain ethnicity as it relates to the plot. Perhaps you are replacing an original cast member and the producer wants the replacement to have the same look and fit the existing costumes. Maybe the director really loves tall, leggy blondes. The scenarios are endless, and they may not always seem fair. But it isn't about "fair"—there is no law that says it has to happen, but typing is here and it's here to stay. You can decide how to feel about it. You can let it make you feel judged and burdened, or you can accept and embrace it. Successful performers not only embrace their type, they own it.

✓ **Physical type:** You need to understand what your type is—in a healthy way. To do that, think objectively, but not judgmentally, as you try this exercise. This will only work if you are honest about your look and abilities. Look at yourself in the mirror. Instead of pointing out your flaws, notice your features. Try to see what others would notice when you walk into an audition room for the first time. What well-known performers do you resemble and what roles have they played? What are the roles that traditionally are cast with performers who look like you? Do you have a look that fits a particular time period, or are you more contemporary? Make a list of the shows you are right for by look alone. These could be plays and musicals but also concert, cruise ship, or theme park shows with which you are familiar. Keep in mind that this list may differ from the list of shows you are dying to do, but that's okay for this exercise. This isn't judgment—it's strategy.

✓ **Skill Set:** Your skill set is a collection of the abilities and talents you possess as a performer. For this next exercise, make a list of the things you do really well. This list should include vocal styling/range, dance genres, dialects, instruments played, special skills—all the things you are well studied in and confident to perform for others. Now make a list of the shows that hire performers with your skills and talents, even if they are shows you don't necessarily want to do. Compare this list to your previous list and look for similarities. You will not only have a list of shows you are right for, but hopefully you will be able to identify the boxes others will want to place you in.

**Accepting your type will ultimately save you frustration**. As much as it helps to know what you are selling, it also helps you to know what you are *not* selling. If you can only sing pop, why audition for a legit operetta? If you are 22 years old, why audition for a role requiring an actress in her 50s? Some shows only hire [insert ethnicity of choice here] because race is pertinent to the story. Some shows only want performers who are [insert height of choice here] because the star is that same height. Typecasting is not personal—it's business. Understanding your type allows you to make wise decisions about what to audition for and how to present yourself in those audition rooms.

**Don't let the boxes limit your artistry.** When you look at the lists you made, realize that you are not stuck with what you see on them. Accepting your type does not mean you will be limited to the same jobs your whole career. Accepting your type does not mean you should lose who you are nor does it mean you can never play your dream role even if you are an untraditional fit. Types do evolve on both sides of the table. As you evolve as an artist, your type can change. Of course, some physical changes can occur. However, and more importantly, your skill set can increase through continued training. You can learn a different style of dance, improve your voice, expand your range, master a dialect, and/or take classes in tumbling and circus.

Remember, versatility breeds opportunity! Having skills that are unique may put you in positions where directors want to create shows around your talents. If you understand the boxes of typecasting, there can also be times where you can change their limited nature. Not every director or writer adheres to strict guidelines. "Colorblind casting[18]" happens. The unions have been instrumental in promoting "non-traditional casting" to diversify work opportunities for all regardless of age, ethnicity, gender, or physical disability. If you decide to audition for a role that you know from your research goes against your type, good for you! Do extensive research on the role, the piece, and the creative team. Be wise about the chance you are taking. Go in armed with information and give them a reason to cast you instead. But go into that room as you—not trying to imitate the type you think they want. You never know what might inspire a director when you are the person walking through the door. If you're good you may very well book the job.

# MARKET ANALYSIS

*Knowledge is power. You have to stay current and know who is doing the work out there when you audition. Art is current and will continue to change. No business is more current than this business.*

**-Lucille DiCampli, partner and agent with bicoastal dance talent agency McDonald/Selznick Associates**

---

[18] Colorblind casting: When directors and producers choose not to let race or ethnicity of a performer become a factor in casting a role. AEA encourages this practice through their "non-traditional casting" campaign. Could also apply to performers who may be deaf, blind, or have some other attribute not historically associated with a particular role.

As a businessperson, it is important to understand the market where you are selling your product. Market analysis is all about gathering information. Knowing about the professional side of the industry will help you understand how you and your brand fit into it. Start now. By evaluating where you currently live, you might discover new opportunities to expand your training or be hired for professional work. You will learn more about your type, the types of jobs that await you, and the names you will need to know as you become a professional. Consider this market analysis a part of your training and practice it often.

- ✓ **Job Opportunities**: There might be more opportunities in the community where you currently live than you think. Make a list of every local opportunity to perform that you know about, whether paid or unpaid. Think in terms of opportunities for adults or older teens, not children. These may include dance companies, community or professional theaters, corporate events, seasonal theme park shows, benefits, chorales, student films, local commercials, or atmospheric dancers for private events or nightclubs. Do some Internet research to find out everything you can about who runs or directs for these companies. Ask your teachers what they know about specific companies. Look in the entertainment listings of your local newspaper or ask people you know who are involved if there are auditions. Can you send in your picture/resume or demo reel to a producer, choreographer or director? Then, get yourself in there, audition and try to get any of these jobs that you can. The more you can learn from the experience of working in your hometown, the more knowledge you will have when you eventually move to a bigger market. You will also have some credits to add to your resume.

- ✓ **Information**: You must find out what is going on in the larger world of professional entertainment, and it couldn't be easier. You have the world of information at your fingertips on the Internet. Start reading! Industry trade websites such as:

    o Backstage/Backstage West (www.backstage.com)
    o Broadway.com (www.broadway.com)
    o Broadway World (www.broadwayworld.com)

   o The Hollywood Reporter (www.hollywoodreporter.com)
   o Playbill (www.playbill.com)
   o Show Business Weekly (www.showbusinessweekly.com)
   o Variety (www.variety.com)

These sites have news articles about what is going on in the business every day. Make a habit of checking them frequently, if not daily. Start to learn the names of directors, choreographers, composers, writers, and producers and what new work they have coming up. To find out what else they have done look them up on:

   o Gypsy's List (www.gypsyslist.com)
   o Internet Broadway Database (www. IBDB.com)
   o Internet Movie Database (www. IMDB.com)

You can learn about industry events, who is casting a particular show, and when the auditions are happening. Even if you cannot attend the audition, read the information anyway. The more informed you are, the better. Knowing what is happening in the market you eventually move to will give you an advantage in gaining a clearer understanding.

✓ **See It:** The third thing you need to do to learn about the market is to actually experience the market! Watch TV. Go see films. Make it a priority to go see live professional theater. Most every community across America has a professional theater within a day's drive, whether it is a dinner theater or a house for Broadway tours. On a trip to a theme park, take the half hour out of your day to catch one of the live shows. Make this investment. Hopefully you'll enjoy the experience, but you should take note of the professional standards and talent levels that these types of jobs require. Pay attention to the technical abilities of the performers. What is their level of training, and is it comparable to your own? Look at other details. Are the women required to perform in heels? Do the dancers also sing? Which performers have features in the show and why? Read the program bios. Who directed and choreographed? Notice which ensemble members understudy the leading roles, and think about why those people were chosen. Experiencing the work will help you to see how your product (type) may or may not fit into specific shows and mediums.

Learning to analyze the profession from the angle of a professional (not just an audience member) will only prepare you more when you are auditioning for jobs in the future.

# SKILL MAINTANENCE / CONTINUED (3) EDUCATION

Just because you have a degree in your hand doesn't mean the training is over. Not only should you be allowing your skill set to evolve to increase your marketability, you need to maintain what you already have. You must be in class, even when you are working steadily as a performer. Find that teacher, coach, or class that speaks to you and make a habit out of going. Work on the skills that need improvement. Study styles and techniques that are new to you. Let new challenges recharge you as an artist. Your art is your product and it must stay fresh and fine-tuned. You'd be surprised how quickly your abilities can diminish from lack of use. Continuing to take class is the best way to keep up your technique and stay in shape, and is also a great way to meet other people in the industry.

Originally from Wichita, Kansas, Yvette Tucker has been working steadily as a union actress and dancer in Los Angeles for more than 15 years. She has played supporting roles in feature films such as *Gangster Squad* and *Miss Congeniality 2*, co-starring roles in television series, and leads at Papermill Playhouse and Pasadena Playhouse. Yvette danced on the Emmys and Grammys with recording artists Christina Aguilera and Shakira as well as on the Emmy-winning special *Tony Bennett: An American Classic* directed by Rob Marshall. She frequently seeks out classes and teachers that help keep her on top of her game.

*Whenever you are in class your creativity is heightened. You are doing the work constantly so auditions don't become your only performances. You won't be going into the audition room rusty. While I was pregnant and knew that I wouldn't be cast for a while, I took the opportunity to learn how to do voiceovers. The class series wasn't just about acting, but about the technical knowledge an actor needs to have to work well in a recording studio. Now that I am back to work, I have a whole new side of the industry available to me.*

Your continued education should not be limited to just physical skill. Knowing the history of your art form as well as the new ideas and trends that will shape the future will keep you working at a more informed level. Performers need to be excellent researchers. Watch archive videos, read biographies, and ask colleagues "who were there" about their experiences. An understanding of production history, time periods, and the work and style of specific composers, directors, and choreographers will help you to prepare for auditions and jobs more effectively. Seeing the performances that are current, both the big-budget work and the experimental "downtown" low-budget pieces, will give you a sense of what the public is buying, where the art form is headed, and how you can stay relevant. And save your ticket stubs—every performance you see counts toward "professional research," which help offset your income taxes for the year.

# NETWORKING

The label of networking can feel "icky" for the person who projects negativity upon it. If that is you, it's time to redefine the meaning of the word. Networking is *not* the practice of trying to get something from someone else, sucking up, or sniveling. Networking is the meeting of industry people in an interested yet non-confrontational way—the building of your own professional business community. This is a crucial part of any small business success. The entertainment world is a small world and "everyone knows everyone" because working professionals are exposed to so many new people each year. Your network building has already begun even if you don't realize it. If you studied your art in school, you already have a group of colleagues who are also now in the industry. You will audition and take classes with any number of other performers in a week. As you begin booking professional jobs, you may end up doing several different gigs within a year, working with different performers, directors, and choreographers each time. Start crunching those numbers and you'll see how easy it is to know a whole lot of folks quickly within the industry— these people become your professional network.

**The relationships you build with other professionals can make a career.** In any profession, it is important to know people in your chosen industry. People like to work with people they "know." They like to recommend people they "know." They trust people they "know." Having a network will lead to more opportunities to be considered for work and, consequently, more work. This concept is not unique to show business, but we are lucky in that we work in a very social industry where meeting people is easier. It is important to have a network of professionals who are performers but also directors, producers, music directors, choreographers, teachers, agents, casting directors, administrators, investors, stage crew, and people who work in all aspects of the industry. No one starts a career with a full network, but you will build it over time.

## WAYS TO NETWORK

- **Meet other performers**. Whether you are in a class, at a special event, at a friend's industry party, etc., make it a point to be social. Knowing other working performers is a great way to learn about auditions and classes, and get recommended to theater companies, choreographers, agents, etc. (word-of-mouth hiring happens often!). It may even help you find a survival job or an apartment to sublet. Want to make a good impression? Don't just talk about yourself and list your resume. Try asking the other person about himself or herself....

- **Audition often.** Getting in front of casting directors and creative teams with good, polished, solid auditions will help people remember you even if you aren't cast in that particular job. The more you do this, the better you become at it. This doesn't mean you should crash every audition whether you are right or not. But you should actively seek out the many opportunities that match your type and skill set.

- **Participate in charity benefits**. Attending industry-specific benefit events for charity, or better yet performing in them, is a great way to meet industry people in an inspired social setting. You also help people who need it—that's even better! There is a balance to participating, however. Beware of becoming so involved in various benefits that you become unavailable for paying work or auditions.

- **Work behind the scenes.** Take industry side jobs: an audition reader for a casting director, an administrative assistant in a talent agent's office, a dancer in a sketch team for a choreographer working on a new piece, a monitor[19] for the holding room of an audition, a volunteer on a union committee, or a representative at someone's trade show industry booth. If you make some money in the meantime, even better.

- **Contact alumni.** If you have trained at a university or conservatory program, get in touch with the successful performers who went through the program ahead of you. Some schools have stronger alumni associations than others, but reaching out to alumni may lead to excellent advice if not working opportunities. You share a common bond.

- **Attend union meetings.** Unions for performers hold membership meetings, talkbacks, and seminars that cover a variety of topics for their members. Get involved. Sometimes they also hold meetings for nonmembers who want to learn more about joining.

- **Go to class.** In the larger cities, many working choreographers teach open dance classes. Directors, agents, and casting directors teach acting and audition technique classes and seminars. Professionals teach in cities across the country on convention and master class tours. Dance captains on national tours teach master

---

[19] Monitor: In this instance, the person who signs performers in and/or calls them into the room at an audition.

classes on the road. Seasoned directors, casting directors, and choreographers teach guest residencies at universities, colleges, and conservatories, and sometimes create shows for community theaters. These opportunities could allow you to meet them personally, show your talent, and possibly be seen by people who are casting. Don't forget to personally thank your teachers after class. Keep up with them later through social media.

- **Stay for the talkback.** At professional theaters and film screenings, there are at times performances or showings followed by an open talkback session. Audience members can learn more about the behind-the-scenes process directly from those involved, and attendance is usually free. You may get to ask questions, learn something new, and meet other professionals.

- **Perform in showcases**. These showings are a chance for young choreographers, directors, and songwriters to have their work seen and heard publicly. Performing in unpaid showcases is great, especially when you are first starting out. If the creative team likes your work, they are also likely to remember you when they eventually book paying work you might be right for. You will also work with other performers and have your work seen by other industry professionals. Showcases are not necessarily going to yield immediate results, but you never know how a positive impression could pay off down the road. Just make sure you keep your priorities in perspective and avoid skipping auditions you are invited to because of showcase scheduling.

- **Schedule informational meetings.** "Informationals" are non-confrontational learning experiences. This is a networking technique that relies on the "six degrees of separation[20]" philosophy and is especially helpful when there is a particular area

---

[20] Six degrees of separation: The philosophy that we are all six or fewer connections away by introduction from every other person on Earth. The idea was hypothesized by Frigyes Karinthy and turned into a popular stage play and feature film.

of the profession you want to work in. For example, let's say your goal is to sing on a cruise ship. Within your network, it is likely you know someone who knows someone else in the industry who has (or is currently) working on a ship. That person could be another singer or a director, casting associate, artistic director, etc. Ask your personal colleague if they will introduce you to that person—not to ask them for a job, but only to learn more about that person's experience and insight. If you make the contact and can talk to that person, find out how they got involved. Ask what skill set their work requires. Knowledge is power, and that is what you should seek. You can't go in expecting to gain an audition, because that puts the person on the spot—only ask to talk. Everybody likes to give advice. Perhaps that person will offer to introduce you to another player in the field so that you can learn more. You also gain the advantage of being put on a particular person's radar.

- **Attend industry parties or events**. If a friend or colleague is involved in a show or film and invites you to attend an opening night or premiere, go! It doesn't matter how big the project is. Accompany your friend to the after party. Meet the creative team involved, the producers, and the managers. Get to know people as human beings without the pressure of being in an audition situation.

- **Stay in touch.** Principles of marketing say you have to see a product seven times for it to enter your consciousness and touch people three times for them to remember you. Share your work with your network. If you are performing in a show or learned a new skill, let people know. If you created a new website or reel or got a new headshot, share it with others. A well-placed email, Facebook message, postcard, or appearance during a person's creative process can work wonders when it comes to someone envisioning you for a current project. Don't overdo it but do keep up-to-date on who is working on what. You can strategically be a presence without being a nuisance.

- **Find a mentor.** It is important to find an older professional in the industry whom you trust—a teacher, director, older performer, or any other industry professional with more knowledge of the business than you. This person will not only be a source of emotional support, but you can bounce your ideas off of them or ask for personal career advice. If you are lucky, this person may also give you access to his or her professional network of contacts, though it is unfair to expect that.

**Don't be afraid to introduce yourself and be yourself.** Meeting someone in a social setting doesn't mean you will end up working together, but then again, someday it might. When meeting someone, no matter what job he or she performs, above all BE GENUINE!! Politeness and manners go a long way. Some performers feel less vulnerable when taking on characters in public. In social situations, a performer might feel the need to be someone they think everyone wants them to be. Morphing into "a public character" can become a coping measure for some when meeting people in the industry. Some markets can perpetuate this other persona—don't buy into it. Being your real self says more about your true character.

**What can you do for me?** This is an unhealthy approach to networking. No one likes a fake—avoid being that person. You never know when the dancer next to you in the audition might become the choreographer of that music video you are hoping to book two years later. You never know when the scene partner you have in Acting 101 might be the director of the new play you audition for 10 years from now. Everyone is on his or her own individual journey, and paths cross again and again. Be smart about how you present yourself. Auditions can become less intimidating when you know—and enjoy the company of—the other people in the room.

David Ruttura has directed new works in New York and regional musicals, and was the associate director for seven Broadway productions including *Lombardi*, *Follies*, and *Spiderman: Turn Off the Dark*. Currently the resident director of *The Phantom of the Opera* national tour, he recommends a healthy approach to networking.

*Networking is important, but networking should be subtle and unobtrusive.*
*You should never be on the make, even though you probably always will be.*
*You have to want to get to know people—there are tons of fascinating, brilliant*
*people in this industry—but you can't and shouldn't always be asking them for*
*a job.*

You won't be successful every time you put yourself out there but the worst thing someone can say to you is "no." Don't take that little word personally or let the fear of it deter you or dictate your career. Just move on and meet someone else. You cannot refrain from putting yourself out there if you intend to get what you want.

# MARKETING

Just like any other product-driven company, you must advertise. Your time in an audition room is never very long. You sing your song, may have a quick chat, and you leave. You learn dance combinations quickly, perform them in groups, and are well out of the room by the time casting decisions are being made. There are tools performers use to promote themselves and be remembered in casting sessions. The most common of these is the headshot and resume—don't underestimate their importance.

## HEADSHOTS

Your professional headshot is one of the most important tools you have to promote your work. Ever eat at a restaurant that advertised itself with a picture of someone tossing his cookies? No. Probably not. They want to turn people on, not turn them away! It is important to use a picture that shows you at your best. Your headshot is your calling card that creative teams are left looking at once you leave the audition room. It is what casting directors use to consider when calling you in. It needs to be a good-quality photo, and it needs to look like you.

You might think a Polaroid is passable or the nice blown-up snapshot your friend took of you in the backyard is good enough to get by. They aren't. My advice: don't do that. Have you heard the phrase "you have to spend money to make money"? It applies in this case. Consider your headshot an investment in your career. Hire a professional headshot photographer with experience shooting for professional performers. A graduation photo or church portrait is *not* a headshot. Headshot photography is an industry unto itself, and the style is completely different from portrait photography. Not just any professional photographer can provide you with what you need.

**You must be strategic about the headshot you choose to use.** You don't want your shot to be too edgy or it will go out of style quickly. You also don't want to be using a black and white print when everyone else is using color. The style of "what's hot and what's not" in headshots changes depending on the market you are auditioning in. Trends differ between New York and L.A. and your market research should include what styles of headshots are current within your chosen medium. The most important thing is that your headshot accurately represents the way you look in the audition room. If you are blonde in your picture but brunette when you walk in the room, you are already preventing the creative team from accurately remembering you when they sit down to cast the show a week later. Plan your shoot strategically by making sure you have a look (hair style, hair color, tan shade/lines, nails, wardrobe, etc.) you plan to maintain for a while. If you get a new look, get a new headshot—by avoiding extreme looks in the first place you can avoid the need to pay for new shots often. You can sometimes use a great headshot up to three or more years if you are lucky and don't vary your look much. That's a lot of use from one session.

Work with a photographer who knows something of the industry and market standards who can coach you appropriately while shooting. The headshot photographer you need may or may not exist in your hometown. If you don't live in a city that has a professional entertainment scene, it will be harder to find a local photographer who can do the job correctly. You might consider getting your headshots done the next time you visit a major-market city. Plan this well in advance—good photographers don't always have last-minute openings. Asking your colleagues for recommendations is a great way to find a photographer and style that is right for you. When narrowing your search, take the time to either meet with potential photographers in person or at the very least talk on the phone. Your comfort level with a person and the way they work can affect the outcome of the photos. Not every photographer is the same—they are artists too. Look at the portfolios on their websites. Make sure their artistic style fits with your style. Go with the photographer whose work you like best and with whom you click well. One amazing shot is what you are ultimately after, but you are likely to get more options if you work well together.

Most headshot photographers offer various packages to choose from, which include a certain number of looks and a certain number of retouched shots. In the digital age, you can expect to receive all of the viable photos from your shoot. Some talented photographers offer great promotional deals, but don't just bargain shop and go with the cheapest option if that person isn't the right fit for you. By the same token, high prices don't always mean they are the best. Including hair and makeup, expect to spend in the range of $400 to $800, give or take. You are investing in yourself.

**The day of the shoot.** Your photographer should give you a list of "dos and don'ts" for your session. These will include wardrobe choices, where to go, and what to bring. Make sure you get plenty of sleep the night before and be well hydrated. Most photographers offer the option of having a hair and makeup professional onsite for both women and men. Some will allow you to bring your own. This is not just a ploy to get you to spend more money. That person is there to help you look your best on camera, avoid the necessity of color correction or removing stray hairs on your favorite shot, and give you another set of artistic eyes to contribute to the creativity of your shoot. He or she is worth the investment.

Think about your type as you prepare for your shoot. Your wardrobe choices, hair, and makeup need to bring out your type but not pin you to a specific character. Don't choose clothing that hides your physique or distracts from your face or complexion. Unless you are creating a modeling portfolio, choosing looks that are too specific to a character type (the goth girl, the uptight businessman, etc.) will limit the frequency with which you can use your shots. For men who like to sport facial hair from time to time, consider doing half of your session with your scruff and the other half clean-shaven. You'll be left with shots that look like you on any given audition day.

After your shoot, you should have many options to choose from. Picking a final shot to use can be difficult. Listen to the recommendations of your photographer and get opinions from others you trust in the industry including directors, choreographers, teachers, agents, and professional performers. Answers may surprise you, and the shot everyone else says looks the most like you might not be your own favorite shot. Be open to suggestions. Unless your grandma works in the industry, she doesn't get the final say! Ultimately, you do get the final say but remember to look at the shot objectively. Does it accurately communicate your type, your personality, and your look? Are your eyes open and sparkling? Will this shot attract people to envisioning you in a variety of job situations?

Getting reproductions (prints) of your headshot is another place you don't want to cut corners. You spent money to get good shots done—don't print them from your color laser printer the night before your audition! Send them to a company that specializes in reproductions of headshots for performers. A search of the trade websites/publications will provide you with several companies to research. The more you get printed, the cheaper they are. Remember, you will give out a lot of pictures each year if you are auditioning frequently so order at least 50 to 100 copies to start. Above all, make sure that your name is printed somewhere on the front side of your reproductions. Some people choose a border and have their name printed within it. Some print it over a corner portion of the photo. Either way, make sure it is easy to see and read. Additionally, make sure you have digital files of your final shot that you can reduce to an easy-to-email size for submitting your headshot online.

## RESUME

Your resume provides creative and casting teams with insight into your experience, background, and training. It lets them know which of their colleagues have also hired and invested in you. If you are good enough to have been hired by one of their friends, you may be good enough to be hired by them!

**What to include:** A performer's resume differs in format from a businessperson's resume in that it is written in a list format rather than curriculum vitae. The information you should include:

✓ **Your Name**: Print it in large bold letters at the top. This is the name of your business—your brand. You want people to notice and remember your name.

✓ **Union Affiliation**: If you are not a member, you don't need to put anything. If you are earning points toward AEA or have enough vouchers, you can put EMC (Equity Membership Candidate) or SAG-Eligible. You'll learn what those terms mean later.

✓ **Contact Info**: If you have an agent, put their contact info. If not, you need to include your mobile number (one that receives voicemail), an email address, and perhaps your website address. Some people choose to create a specific email address they reserve only for professional correspondence.

  o **Contact info is imperative**. How is someone supposed to offer you a job if they can't get in touch with you? Make sure you have voicemail with a clear outgoing message. Make sure it is working. If there is a period of time when you will be unable to check your voicemail (international travel, out-of-range vacation), record a new outgoing message indicating that callers should contact you via email during that period.

✓ **Stats**: Height and vocal range—these are helpful to a casting team later on as they try to recall things about you. Hair/eye color are optional as headshots are now in color. You do not need to include your weight or age. Many people also include a small headshot embedded in the upper corner for easy recognition.

✓ **Credits**: Bigger credits should be placed toward the top of your resume regardless of the dates they occurred. If auditioning for a film/TV job, you should list those credits before theater. Vice versa for a theater or stage audition. It is not uncommon to have a couple different versions of your resume depending upon the market/medium you are auditioning in. Tailor your resume to the job you are auditioning for—this is a basic business principle that applies to many industries.

- o Credits should be separated by categories. These might include National Tours, Regional Theater, Summer Stock, Film, Television, Industrials, New York Theater, Dance, Commercials, Educational Theater, Theme Park/Cruise Line, Community Theater, etc.

- o Your role (middle column) can list the character name, type of role (lead, ensemble, supporting, etc.), and related information such as understudy (written usually as "u/s"), swing, dance captain, or standby. If you actually went on in the role you understudied, you may write "covered/performed" after the role name.

✓ **Training**: It helps people to know where you have trained and with whom. Some schools carry excellent reputations in the industry, and showing that you studied there could work in your favor. Including names will help a creative team discover if you have mutual colleagues in common.

✓ **Special Skills:** This line can help the panel if they need something specific for a project. It can also become a conversation starter in the audition room. Only include skills that you actually do well and that you would be willing to perform. If you don't tumble—or you can but would prefer not to—then don't write "tumbling."

The following are basic examples of standard resume formats. Notice details like how to list directors, clean alignment of the columns, ways to list your teachers, and more. You do not need to label the columns (Show, Role, Venue), as industry people will understand what information is where.

## Resume Format #1

# JANE DOE
### EMC

Height: 5'4       Cell: 818-555-1234
Vocal range: Mezzo (A - B$b$)       janedoe@email.com
Hair: Blonde / Eyes: Green       www.janedoeactress.com

**REGIONAL THEATRE**

| | | |
|---|---|---|
| The Taming of the Shrew | Bianca | Shakespeare In The Park |
| | | dir. Tom Sawyer |
| West Side Story* | Jet Girl/Ensemble | Classics Theater Company |
| *original Robbins choreography | | dir. Tom Sawyer |
| Hair | Ensemble | Downtown Theatre Space |
| | | choreo. Moll Flanders |

**EDUCATIONAL THEATRE**

| | | |
|---|---|---|
| Bye Bye Birdie | Kim MacAfee | University of Somewhere |
| Hamlet | Ophelia | University of Somewhere |
| I Love You, You're Perfect Now Change | Girl 1 | University of Somewhere |
| The Glass Menagerie | Laura u/s | University of Somewhere |
| | | guest dir. Nancy Drew |
| Oklahoma! | Swing/Dance Capt. | University of Somewhere |

**FILM**

| | | |
|---|---|---|
| For a Living | Anne (lead) | student film |

**DANCE**

| | | |
|---|---|---|
| The Nutcracker | Chinese/Snow Corps | Starz Dance Company |
| American Cancer Society Benefit | Dancer | Downtown Theatre Space |

**TRAINING**
BFA in Theatre: University of Somewhere
    Acting: Sam Spade (Meisner & scene study), Daisy Buchanan (classical)
    Voice: Max Caufield, Elizabeth Bennett, Elinor Dashwood
    Dance: Moll Flanders (Jazz & Tap), Hedda Gabler (Ballet), Shere Khan (Modern)
Aerial Silks and Trapeze (1 year)—Circus Arts Center
Starz Dance Studio (St. Louis, MO)—7 Years Jazz, Ballet/Pointe, Tap, Hip-Hop
    Master Classes: Tom Ripley, Bill Sykes, Patrick Bateman

**SPECIAL SKILLS**
Aerial silks, Tumbling, Horseback Riding, Tennis, Skiing, Salsa and Swing Dancing

## Resume Format #2

# JANE DOE

COLOR
HEADSHOT
HERE

818-555-1234  www.janedoeactress.com
janedoe@email.com
Vocal range: Mezzo (A - B♭)

Height: 5'4 / Hair: Blonde

### FILM / TELEVISION

| | | |
|---|---|---|
| Main Street Café commercial | lead | local / Small Town Prod. |
| For a Living | Anne (lead) | student film / U. of S. |

### THEATER / STAGE

| | | |
|---|---|---|
| The Taming of the Shrew<br>dir. Tom Sawyer | Bianca | Shakespeare In The Park |
| West Side Story<br>dir. Tom Sawyer | Ensemble | Classics Theater Company |
| Hairspray<br>choreo. Moll Flanders | Ensemble/Featured dancer | Downtown Theatre Space |
| Bye Bye Birdie | Kim MacAfee | University of Somewhere |
| Hamlet | Ophelia (covered/performed) | University of Somewhere |
| I Love You, You're Perfect, Now Change | Girl 1 | University of Somewhere |
| The Glass Menagerie<br>guest dir. Nancy Drew | Laura u/s | University of Somewhere |
| Oklahoma! | Swing/Dance capt. | University of Somewhere |
| The Nutcracker | Chinese/Snow corps | Starz Dance Company |

### INDUSTRIAL

| | | |
|---|---|---|
| American Cancer Society Benefit | Dancer | Downtown Theatre Space |

### TRAINING

BFA in Theater: University of Somewhere
> Acting: Sam Spade (Meisner & scene study), Daisy Buchanan (classical)
> Voice: Max Caufield, Elizabeth Bennett, Elinor Dashwood
> Dance: Moll Flanders (Jazz & Tap), Hedda Gabler (Ballet), Shere Khan (Modern)

Shakespeare Theater Center Summer Intensive
Master Classes: Tom Ripley, Bill Sykes, Patrick Bateman

### SPECIAL SKILLS

Clarinet, Roller skating, Horseback riding, Tennis, Skiing, Salsa and Swing dancing

**What NOT to include:** Common things on a business resume that you *should not* include on a performance resume are:

- ✓ A job objective (You want to perform! Why else would you be auditioning?)
- ✓ Work dates (Bigger credits are listed toward the top regardless of date.)
- ✓ General duties/skills a role required (List your role and if you were also an understudy, swing, or dance captain. We don't need to know you cried on cue or square danced.)
- ✓ Your age, if you are over 18 (Type means more to them than your actual age.)
- ✓ <u>Do not</u> list your home address or your Social Security number (This protects you should your resume fall into the wrong hands.)
- ✓ Unrelated work experience, or nonperformance theater jobs (Technical experience is important only if you are applying for a technical job. Your retail job is not pertinent.)

People behind the table are familiar with the standard industry format. The more you ask a panel to search your resume to locate pertinent information, the less time they are going to spend actually watching your audition. You want their eyes on you. Following this format keeps information clearly organized. Directors and casting directors can find what they need quickly.

**Always limit your performance resume to one page.** Resumes are about quality, not quantity. As you accumulate more professional credits, you can begin to take the amateur and educational credits off. Listing every show you have done since age five doesn't present you as more appealing or more qualified. Tiny print is hard to read quickly. Too much information on a resume will cause the auditor to spend more time reading and less time watching your actual audition.

Your headshot should be stapled (preferably all four corners) or glued to the backside of your resume.

Creative teams notice the details—a sloppy resume is a pet peeve. It communicates a sense that the performer doesn't pay attention to details, is unorganized, or just doesn't care. Take the extra time to make sure all of your columns are perfectly lined up, that names of directors and choreographers are spelled correctly, and that the paper is clean with edges trimmed to line up perfectly with your headshot—letter-sized paper is larger than the standard 8x10-sized headshot. Your resume represents your product/brand. If you walked into a copy store and noticed that all the signs behind the counter had crooked typesetting, would you trust them to make a sign for you? Greatness lies in the details.

After you create your resume, print it out and proofread it vigorously. Make sure your contact information is accurate. Update your resume so it is always a current reflection of your work. Avoid handwriting in new credits—take a minute to get on your computer and add that credit in with the proper formatting.

The most important thing regarding resumes: DO NOT LIE! Don't print false information. Don't say you were in a show if you weren't. Don't say you worked with a director if you didn't. It may not happen at your first audition, but I promise you that eventually YOU WILL GET CAUGHT. And it won't be pretty. Your reputation is everything, and you don't want to be known as the person who lies on his/her resume. People remember that!

## WEBSITE

An online presence is essential for today's working performer. Many professionals opt to create a website to represent them artistically and professionally. A personalized website allows you to keep your current information accessible. A new credit, a new skill, a new photo, a new agent—you can present it all on your own page. Potential employers can view your body of work instantly. Casting directors are using a performer's online presence more and more for audition prescreening. Most businesses today have a website, so why wouldn't you?

Whether you hire a graphic designer or create a simple site on your own, the biggest priorities should be that it loads quickly and is easy to navigate. Just like your resume, your website must prominently display your name and a way to contact you or your representatives. Use your headshot and some additional shots from your professional photo shoot in the design. If you have permission, include production photos and video clips of yourself from previous work. Make sure that your resume and headshot are on there, easy to find, and in downloadable formats (pdf and jpg) for casting directors and employers. These formats also ensure that the careful alignment on your resume stays intact. Include embedded videos or links to you in performance, even if you are only in a studio, but remember to thoughtfully control the product people will see—only upload footage that shows you at your very best. This is still advertising! Other optional features are a short bio, published reviews that mention you favorably, latest news announcements, audio vocal selections, and perhaps a professional blog.

When securing your domain name, purchase one with your professional name in it. Register your site with Google and other search engines so that it comes up first when people search for your name. Your website address should be on your resume, business cards, Facebook page, program bios, and anywhere else you promote yourself professionally.

## SOCIAL MEDIA

Popular social media sites including Facebook, Twitter, and LinkedIn are tools to use to your advantage. You can easily keep your network updated with what you are doing professionally—connecting through social media to the people who hire means they are likely to see your name and face more often. It also allows you to stay connected to what is happening in the industry. Projects coming down the line, networking events, audition notices, talent recommendations—as your network grows to include more creatives and employers, you will see all of these scrolling across your feed.

Be wise about social media—careless use can just as easily hurt you. Any statements or photos you post are accessible by these same potential employers. Remember this and think *before* you post! People might just take a look at your Facebook page prior to hiring you. The photos of you drinking and partying at 3 a.m. might not make the best first impression. Past or current employers will not appreciate you venting about them in public status updates. Talking about a job you are going to do before interested parties have announced the project to the public could get you in trouble. Likewise, posting about the acceptance of one job before informing interested parties that you are turning down another job they offered you won't help your reputation. Anything you put on the Internet is accessible to the public at any time—be smart. You can take steps to control your public image and still live a personal life by using your privacy settings to control who can see what, untagging yourself, or taking down photos of a questionable nature. You may even have separate pages to represent yourself professionally and connect with your family and close friends.

Not all companies or people prefer to be contacted or have submissions sent through social media sites, so do your best to research personal preferences. If a company or individual lists a website or specific email address, they are indicating that is their preferred method for professional correspondence.

If you choose to use social media for professional networking, consider the following tips:

- **Status Update Tip #1**—"I got called in for this. I got called in for that." Every time you have an invited audition or callback, you don't need to post about it. Your industry colleagues will become annoyed. Tell your family and friends personally about your auditions if you choose, but your entire network doesn't need the details. Keep it in perspective—you might think these posts present you as successful, but they can just as easily come across as boastful or backhanded. Every performer has auditions. It's what we do. Does an electrician post every time he changes a light bulb? Regardless of intent, perception is everything. Telling a funny story about an audition mishap or the job you are beginning is completely different.

- **Status Update Tip #2**—Don't flood everyone's news feeds. Posting updates too frequently is a great way to encourage other professionals to block you from their news feeds, which, in turn, diminishes your ability to market yourself effectively and defeats the purpose.

- **Status Update Tip #3**—A little mystery can be intriguing. Resist the urge to make all of the details of your life and career completely transparent. You can stay in people's consciousness without offering "too much information." Humor and inspirational posts can draw people in just as much, or more, than endless posts that are all about you, your life, and your feelings.

## AUDIO/VISUAL SOCIAL MEDIA

Creating your own page on YouTube or Vimeo to showcase your talent will boost your marketing range. Put together a performance reel and make it the centerpiece of your page. Reels are a 2:30 to 4:00-minute long compilation of you dancing, singing, and/or acting a role in performance on stage or film, in rehearsal, and/or in class. It might consist of clips from professional or student films or web series you have done. Post additional clips of longer scenes, full songs, and complete pieces to keep your "Channel" current. Don't forget to make your page visually match your brand. Professionally edited reels can give you that extra marketing edge— you can expect to pay a few hundred dollars—but the computer savvy often make their own.

Casting directors frequently look to YouTube or Vimeo pages when considering whether or not to call in an actor whom they don't know for an audition. Cruise line, theme park, and theater production companies have been known to hire a dancer or singer directly from viewing his or her performance reel. There are even notorious instances when Broadway productions have found performers or specialty acts for Broadway shows through a YouTube search—though it has happened only in rare and very specific instances….

Only post videos showcasing your most exceptional work! Remember, you have control over what people see with your name on it—show them your product at its best.

## DATABASE PROFILES

Online databases with talent profiles are searched daily by any number of casting directors. Each actor's profile includes headshots, credits, and resume and perhaps related videos, archive photos, links to websites, and biographical information.

**Actors Access** (www.actorsaccess.com), created by Breakdown Services,[21] lists those actors represented by franchised talent agents. Non-represented performers may also apply independently for inclusion. To search for talent on Actors Access, one must have an exclusive membership. Most casting directors in the major markets agree to the importance of being listed on this database, as they rely on it often.

**The Internet Movie Database** (www.imdb.com) is a public database that lists all professionals (not just actors) engaged in the film and television industry. Performers pay to create a personal page. An IMDB page gives you yet another searchable online presence, and it is a great research tool for you to learn more about directors and other professionals.

## MAILINGS/EMAILINGS

Sending a hardcopy (preferred by most) or an email with attachments of your picture and resume, along with a cover letter, to casting directors for specific projects is a way to be noticed prior to an audition or be invited in for consideration. When you are in a show, sending a postcard to personally invite a casting director or agent might get them out to see you. Their business is finding performers, so letting them know how to find you actually makes their jobs easier. Only invite them if you and the work are good. The legitimate offices have published mailing and email addresses online and in annual printed listings. Many performers have resorted to only emailing their submissions in order to save time, resources, and money. This is still a tricky practice. With the hundreds of emails casting directors and agents receive each day, many emailed submissions are left unopened or deleted—but they still open their mail from the post office. Never underestimate the importance of sending your information "old school" and trust that when casting directors and agents want an email submission, they will post a notice and request it. Learn each person's preference.

---

[21] Breakdown Services: an online business used by casting directors and agents for theater, film, TV, and commercial talent submissions.

## BUSINESS CARDS

Business cards in your wallet come in handy. Opportunities for networking with other professionals will arise at random times; for example, you might be just the right type of person for a project someone is working on. Business cards provide the recipient with a way to remember you once the conversation has ended. Business cards should include your name, contact info, and website address. For performers, using your headshot in the design makes your brand, and face, more memorable. Online companies make designing and printing your cards easy and cheap.

## POSTCARDS/THANK YOU NOTES

Prior to the Internet age, sending a thank you note on a postcard in the mail to a casting director or director/choreographer after an audition was an industry standard. The card generally included the performer's headshot, name, and contact number on the front and a personal note on the back reminding the recipient of the project they were seen for along with thanks for the opportunity. Don't forget, most of the higher-ups in this business once knew this as a standard practice. Respect that. Sometimes a handwritten thank you note can go a very long way. Try not to ask for something when you thank the person. Be genuine. Some managers and agents prefer to receive postcards from prospective clients as well.

## EMAIL BLASTS

Creating a database of your industry contacts and sending out email blast updates about what you are doing is also tricky. Some recipients will appreciate reading something quick regarding your recent accomplishments or may want to attend your upcoming showcase. You may jump to the front of their consciousness. Others will consider it spam mail and delete it without reading it—some may become annoyed. You never know. Frequency is the key. A blast every week, or even every month, is too much. Every four or five months is better but still may be too often for some recipients. Though email blasts can be a way to stay in the consciousness of potential employers and casting directors, you should always:

✓ Ask to add a recipient.

✓ Include an "unsubscribe" option for recipients, and honor it when someone no longer wishes to receive group emails. Don't take it personally.

✓ Use the "bcc" feature so that your entire contact list is not broadcast to all recipients.

✓ By all means, only write a blast when you truly have something substantial to share.

## TEXTING

Don't do it. Texting is not an appropriate way to market yourself. Ten years from now, who knows? For now, stay away from it. Reserve texting for communicating with your close friends and family members, or colleagues who invite you to text. Presumed texting is too informal and puts people on the spot for an immediate response. You never know when your text might cost the recipient money. Stick to the mediums listed above for now when it comes to marketing.

 # STRATEGY

Knowing your brand and market, continually improving your product, networking, and marketing yourself will all pave the way for opportunity to strike. No one does any of this perfectly when they first start out, but make the effort and learn from your mistakes. You will continue to get better at it as your career progresses.

Director David Ruttura didn't just wait around for chance to take him to Broadway. By putting himself out there with a smart and proactive approach, he set himself up for opportunity to strike when the timing was right.

*There's a tremendous amount of luck involved with this business, whether you've made it or are trying to. But with all things, luck doesn't just happen. It needs to be tempered by an individual thinking about where they need to be and when, who they need to know and why, and how they can meet them. Everyone in this business has an ego, and those egos can be stroked to your advantage. It sounds cynical, but simply finding someone you respect and admire and figuring out a way to get in contact with them, not for a job per se, but just to get their advice on something, lays a foundation for luck to jump on.*

You are entering a business that offers no guarantees, where you are subject to many factors beyond your control. You won't always receive feedback to guide you and the hustle for work never ends—even the biggest stars have to pitch themselves for projects. That doesn't mean you can't follow a business strategy. There are performers achieving their goals every day despite the uncertainty of the business. Use your small business tools to control the elements you can—you do get the choice to say yes or no in the end and can choose the career trajectory you want to focus on.

- **Set real business goals for yourself.** Long- and short-term goals are all relevant. Make a dream list of the roles you'd love to play or shows you'd like to be in and a bucket list of the types of jobs you hope to book across your career. Make a second list of practical goals that will better your career: becoming a proficient tap dancer, attending a union informational meeting, auditioning for a particular theater or director, reading and understanding more Shakespeare, studying with a certain teacher, etc. Accept that the timing of accomplishments on the first list will be left to opportunity striking, but understand you have much more choice over the timing of things on the second list. Start working your second list into your real calendar.

- **Keep track of your journey.** Maintaining an audition journal with names of projects, companies, directors, choreographers, and casting directors you've auditioned for, along with what you sang, what you wore, if you were called back, etc., is a way you can chart your progress. You will begin to see trends in what works for you consistently (wardrobe, song choice, types of roles) and what doesn't while keeping track of how you know people. This can benefit your networking skills. You are more apt to remember someone when you cross paths again at a later date because you took the extra time to record the experience.

- **Associate with the world you seek.** You might not control when you will land your dream job, but you can use your network to find the circles of people working in the genre that interests you. Meeting and/or associating with these people will lead to greater knowledge and understanding of what it takes to do what they do. It may take some time for this to happen, but linear goals like expanding your network and being a presence in a specific circle of people will give you a marker for success besides just the jobs you've done.

- **Do something for your business every day.** You may not have a performance, an audition, or a class every day, but that doesn't mean you can't be open for business anyway. It could be as simple as sending an email, submitting a resume and picture, reading a trade website, or going to yoga, but make it a point to do at least one thing for your career each day. Every time you put yourself out there, become more informed, or better your artistry, you are helping the growth of yourself and your business.

- **Remember there is power in a well-placed email.** Be strategic about your communications through social media, uploads, and correspondence. Help those who hire to remember you, and chances are they just might when the time is right.

- **Refresh your vision.** Once a year, really sit down and re-evaluate where you are. Did you reach the goals you set for the year? Are you growing as an artist? Were you distracted by other opportunities? Is there a new medium you want to pursue? Refocus as you move forward. Know when to say "no".

Kristen Coury, the founder and producing artistic director of the Gulfshore Playhouse, an Equity theater in Naples, Florida, says that if this is your passion you need to go for it. But be serious about it.

*It's not an easy business. That part I'm sure I don't have to tell you. But here's the thing I'm sure not everyone is going to say: DO IT. Despite years of hitting walls, searching for my niche, working for peanuts, and all the rest, there was never a time when I seriously considered getting out of this glorious business. I work every day with the goal of expressing art that will make peoples' lives better. And I get to do it with other artists who are as crazily passionate about what they do as I am. Doesn't get much better than that. So it's worth it—but: DO IT LIKE YOU MEAN IT. I've seen actors show up for auditions having never looked at the sides. I've heard interns say they don't like two-show days because the days are too long. Bottom line: if you're not going to bring all your energy to the table, put your whole heart and soul into this endeavor, and give it all you got, don't bother. This business is too hard, too demanding, and requires too much time and sacrifice to be here if you don't LOVE IT. So memorize the sides and show up for the audition in an outfit vaguely reminiscent of the character you'd love to play, get everything before the director is breathing down your neck, and be mindful of the fact that you could be working that 10-hour day behind the counter of a retail establishment but you're in a theatre instead. If you LOVE IT, stick with it. Have no fear. There'll be a place for you. The reward will be the gift of getting to work in one of the best professions ever.*

Four

# Auditions

Auditions: they are a part of the business you either love or hate or love to hate. The act of putting yourself, your work, your artistry out there for others to instantly judge is one of the hardest parts of being a professional. There's no way around it, though; the act of auditioning is how we book jobs, and it is here to stay.

Make the decision to go in with positive energy. The chance to be in a room learning choreography from some of the best dance makers in the world can be very exciting, even if you don't get the job. The chance to consider notes[22] from an accomplished director can help you grow. Nobody gets every job they audition for, and even the biggest stars in the world still have to audition. You are not alone—we are all in the same boat. Just get out there, put your best foot forward, don't dwell on the negative, and hope for the best.

## AUDITION TECHNIQUE

Auditioning is a skill. It takes practice to be able to show your level of talent and uniqueness in a short amount of time. Auditions add a level of stress and anxiety that must be managed as you present your work. They require trusting immediate instincts and an ability to learn new material

---

[22] Note: A critique or request given to a performer from a member of the creative team or a stage manager/dance captain. Notes can be given about anything within or relating to the performance and are generally given in the spirit of what is best for the show, character, and overall artistic vision.

quickly. Audition techniques for film or commercials differ from audition techniques for vocalists or theater. You can't become good at auditioning by reading a book—the art of auditioning well is a skill that needs to be physically learned and physically practiced. Notes on audition technique are best when tailored to the individual. Most college programs and studio/conservatory scholarship programs offer courses, workshops, or seminars in how to give a successful audition. Taking classes in auditioning from casting directors, agents, directors, coaches, and other professionals will help you to be more prepared. These classes are offered in major markets on a consistent basis and are regularly advertised in the trades. As a professional, you need to add audition technique classes to your personal training syllabus.

New York actress Pamela Bob watched as her classmates from the University of Cincinnati College-Conservatory of Music (CCM) began landing Broadway shows one by one while she couldn't get arrested by the very same casting directors hiring them.

> *I still am kicking myself for not having taken a musical theatre audition class early on in my career. I was too afraid to get up in front of a class and "fail." It took years, literally, for me to build up the courage to get in an audition class. When I finally did, the experience changed my life and my career. It gave me a new confidence that I had been lacking. (I'm still kicking myself!)*

Since enrolling in audition classes and studying to improve her skills, Pamela has played lead roles in New York both on Broadway and off-Broadway. Getting over her fears has allowed her more opportunities to let her many talents shine on stage.

In addition to helping you present your talents at their best, classes in how to audition will teach you about the mechanics of auditioning, such as effectively introducing yourself ("slating"), working with the accompanist, assessing your environment, how and where to stand when you sing, etc. Learning by doing in class is better than flailing around an audition room unprepared. Business professionals take seminars on how to interview effectively—this is our version. You are not automatically bestowed with audition instincts just because you are a talented performer. The best performers are not always the best auditioners, and the best auditioners are not always the best performers.

Emmy-nominated choreographer and director Patti Colombo has choreographed series for The Disney Channel, the Broadway revival of *Peter Pan* starring Cathy Rigby, national tours of *Seussical* and *Teenage Mutant Ninja Turtles*, and productions in the U.K., Japan, and Russia. Before she was a choreographer and director, however, she was a dancer and actress in film and television in L.A., and played "Val" on Broadway in *A Chorus Line*.

> *I used to either audition really well and get the job or so terribly that I would be cut immediately. If I listened at the door and heard someone who sang better than me, I would start to judge myself. When you are just starting out, go to as many auditions as you can (that you are right for) so that you become comfortable with it and the less afraid and vulnerable you will be. You have to learn to not let insecurities get in your own way. Stay in classes. Keep learning because there are incredibly talented people out there and you have got to stay on top of the game. It's exhausting but you've got to do it.*

Learning audition technique that will help you present yourself at your best should be a priority. Get in class.

# TYPES OF AUDITIONS

There are various types of audition calls[23] that offer different levels of accessibility for performers to be seen. Casting does happen from each type of call.

- **Invited Calls:** This term is more common for theater/stage and dance auditions. These are closed auditions where specific performers must be invited to audition. For some projects, only

---

[23] Call: (1) an audition is also referred to as an "audition call." Sometimes it is just shortened to "call"; i.e., "They are having a call for that show."(2) as in "call time." The exact time performers are expected to be at work and ready to begin. "The stage manager gave actors their calls for the next day."(3) as in "call the show." The act of a stage manager giving audible and visual cues to the crew during a performance while following their prompt book.

agents and managers are asked to submit clients for consideration. Casting directors narrow down these submissions and only call in those they feel are right. Directors and choreographers submit a list of specific performers they would like to see. Casting directors may also call people in from their own files that they have prescreened to be right for a project. It may take you some time as you develop in your career before you start getting called for invited auditions. That is normal and a part of becoming established.

- **Pre-Reads:** If a casting director has an interest in an actor, but does not yet know his or her work/talent or whether he or she is right for a particular role, they may invite that actor in for a private audition, or "pre-read." This is a pre-screening process for the casting director so that they know an actor's abilities prior to putting them in front of a creative team at a callback. Pre-reads are more common in film/television.

- **Open Submissions**: Some casting notices ask performers to submit a headshot, resume, and possibly a reel either via email or regular mail. Sometimes casting is done from these submissions, but most times the casting director chooses whom to call in based on those submissions.

- **Union Calls**: For stage work, not all auditions are invite only, but some are restricted to union members only. The union agreements mandate that producers hold a certain number of required calls for each production that are open to all union members where members are seen first. If a union member shows up to a call before the start time, he or she is guaranteed to be seen.

- **Open Calls**: These calls are open to all interested performers. Also called "cattle calls," these tend to be well attended, as they are accessible to all performers, both union and non-. The stories you hear about "the line around the block" generally take place at open calls. Most jobs looking for non-union talent will search through open calls.

- **Callbacks:** A callback is when you are asked to return for a second or third audition after attending the initial call. Sometimes a performer will wear the same audition outfit they wore to the initial audition to help a creative team recognize him or her. You don't have to do this, but some people are of the belief that it helps and works for them. (You can decide for yourself.) You may be asked to learn a specific song or sides[24] either prior to or at the actual callback. You will be asked to read for one or more specific characters. You will either have a reader provided to read opposite of you in the room or you may be paired up with a fellow auditioner.

  If dancing, you might perform the same combination as before, learn a new one, do some partnering, or be asked to improvise in certain commercial situations. Singers may be asked to vocalize to hear range, learn specific parts from a song, again perform their original audition selection, or read for roles as an understudy[25]. For film, you may do a screen test performing memorized sides with or without another actor. For television pilots, you may have to perform for studio or network executives and/or do a screen test. Performers can go through one or several callbacks for one job. Per contractual rules, union members may be paid if asked to come back in more than a specified number of times. (This is rare.)

One detail about union calls for stage work that non-union talent aren't told off the bat is that non-union talent might have the chance to be seen at a union call even though they have not yet joined. Most regional and stock theaters with union agreements require their creative teams to hire a mixed cast of union and non-union performers. The economic climate makes it very hard for theater companies to afford all union casts, so Actors' Equity has granted concessions of a predetermined ratio of union to non-union contracts within a production. This means those casting need

---

[24] Sides: a cutting of dialogue from the script of the project you are auditioning for.

[25] Understudy: Someone who learns a lead or principal role in addition to his/her own role. An understudy performs if the regular actor must miss a performance for any reason. Also called a "cover" or sometimes "standby," though standbys generally do not perform any other track.

to find non-union talent to fill those available slots in addition to finding the union talent. To do this, creative teams often see non-union talent at union calls after all of the union talent has auditioned and if time permits.

If you are non-union, you can show up to union-only calls. It will involve waiting around for some time to be seen and you might not be seen at all, but the risk can potentially pay off in the end. When you book a job in a union house, you can accrue the Equity Membership Candidate (EMC) points you will need to join the union (to be explained later). This is helpful if you wish to pursue union jobs and eventually join the union.

Sometimes performers show up to invited calls when they have not actually been invited. Hoping to be seen anyway, they ask the casting director or monitor to allow them into the room to audition. This is called "crashing" the call. It puts people in an awkward position. Invited calls are usually invite only for a reason—if the casting director knows who you are, there may be a reason you weren't called in. If he or she doesn't know you, you are putting them on the spot by asking and might not be making the best impression. You should consider professional relationships prior to crashing an invited call. I can't say people haven't booked jobs through crashing, but I can tell you how their colleagues perceive them. At times, during open or union calls, men have been known to crash women's calls and vice versa due to availability. This is different. If time allows for it, a monitor, casting director, or creative team usually does not have a problem seeing someone.

# FINDING AUDITIONS

When a project is ready to be cast, the casting directors and producers release an audition notice called a breakdown. A breakdown is a listing that includes the name of the project, dates of rehearsals and performances or anticipated shoot days, union affiliation, names of the creative team, location/time of the auditions, what to bring, and specifics about the characters and types they are looking to cast.

Auditions for film and television are usually granted through agent submissions only. Breakdowns posted on The Breakdown Service database for invited calls are accessible only to franchised agents (though some connected actors have been known to gain access to the service for themselves…networking, anyone?). Auditions for live stage shows and student films are often listed openly and casting directors publish breakdowns for non-invited calls in a variety of accessible places.

## ONLINE TRADES[26]/PUBLICATIONS

In the Internet age, finding auditions has never been easier. Most production companies post their audition notices on one or more of the online trades. Audition websites, like those listed here, have replaced most of the weekly or monthly printed trade papers. The larger the market, the more likely auditions will appear on one of the trade websites. Though new websites pop up all the time, some of the more established sites include:

- **ActorsAccess.com:** A database where you can create a profile that casting directors can use to search for talent. You can also use the site to submit yourself to be considered for projects. Membership requires an application.

- **ActorsEquity.org:** The official website for Actors' Equity Association lists the Equity Chorus Calls (ECCs) and Equity Principle Auditions (EPAs) for all stage jobs that fall under an Equity contract. They list the union auditions occurring in all cities.

- **Answers4Dancers.com:** Created by renowned dancer and choreographer Grover Dale, this is an excellent resource geared toward young professional dancers. There is a membership fee. Audition notices tend to seek dancers specifically, though they also include auditions for musical theater performers. There are also great resources and articles written by industry insiders.

---

[26] Trades: Publications and websites that are specific to an industry, but not specifically applicable or interesting to the general public.

- **Backstage.com:** *Backstage* still prints a weekly newspaper; however, accessing their online site allows you the most up-to-date listings. There is a membership fee. Audition notices are comprehensive, covering both union and non-union stage, film and television; open calls, theme parks and cruise lines, casino shows, and more. *Backstage* lists auditions taking place in New York, Los Angeles, Chicago, Las Vegas, and most other large markets in the U.S.

- **Dance Magazine & Pointe Magazine:** These long-established publications create yearly listings of auditions for professional dance companies across the U.S. as well as international companies.

- **LeagueOfChicagoTheatres.com & TheatreInChicago.com:** Both of these sites list auditions taking place in Chicago and the surrounding areas. *Theatre In Chicago* will also lead you to links for sister sites that list auditions in the Boston, D.C., L.A., New York, Minneapolis, Seattle, San Francisco, and Atlanta markets.

- **Playbill.com & Broadwayworld.com:** These sites mainly serve as online industry magazines/news outlets, but also have pages with audition notices.

- **StageDoorAccess.com:** A paid membership site where you can create an online profile and browse audition notices for a variety of markets.

- **VegasAuditions.com:** Lists all auditions for the Las Vegas market. There is a membership fee.

## COMPANY WEBSITES

When searching for information about specific theater, production, entertainment, or dance companies you have interest in auditioning for, a browsing of their official company website should provide you with a who's who list, as well as upcoming seasons, audition schedules, and online submission policies. Company websites are the best resources for finding out about local auditions being held.

## AUDITION CONFERENCES

Outside of the major markets, there are ways to audition for several theater and production companies in one setting. Conference organizations hold annual audition conferences for registered performers to attend. Some charge a registration fee and offer classes and seminars in addition to audition opportunities. Generally, performers audition with prepared songs and monologues, and learn a dance combination in front of a panel of casting and artistic directors representing several companies. Each company calls back only those performers they are interested in seeing more from later in the weekend. Theater conferences are great for pre-professional college theater and dance majors looking to book summer stock, theme park, and other work between semesters or immediately following graduation.

Some of the more popular and established conferences include:

- Southeastern Theatre Conference (www.setc.org)
- New England Theatre Conference (http://netconline.org)
- Unified Professional Theatre Auditions (www.upta.org)
- StrawHat Auditions (www.strawhat-auditions.com)
- Florida Professional Theatres Association (www.fpta.net)
- Midwest Theatre Auditions
  (www.webster.edu/fine-arts/midwest-theatre-auditions)

The conference websites have specific information about what they offer and which producing organizations will be attending. Further researching those attending organizations will help you to prepare for the specific upcoming seasons you will be auditioning for.

## BULLETIN BOARDS

Professional dance studios, acting schools, and rehearsal studios usually have public bulletin boards where producers, directors, and choreographers post audition notices seeking a variety of performers. You should take extra care to check into the background of a project you find posted on a bulletin board.

## WORD OF MOUTH

Reach out to your network. Learning about auditions and submission opportunities via word of mouth is certainly effective.

# FREQUENTLY ASKED QUESTIONS

**What does a casting director do?**

Casting directors are an intricate part of the casting process. Their main objective is to find talent and put viable options for all roles in front of the creative team. In an industry with an extraordinarily large number of performers, narrowing down the right people for the right job is no easy task. Casting directors keep extensive files on the talent pools in their markets and constantly search for new talent. They tend to specialize in certain types of work, whether it is musical theater, commercials, television, etc. However, some larger casting offices may handle many different types of projects.

The casting director works with the director and producer to create the breakdown. He or she will get the breakdowns into the trades and onto the Breakdown Service for agents and will then organize and run all casting sessions and auditions from start to finish. During open calls, casting directors work to find the few among the many who could be right and then call them back to be seen by the creative team. For invited calls, casting directors consult with agents, managers, and their own files to call in the specific types needed for a project. During the audition process, casting directors act as liaisons between the creative teams and actors to make sure that actors have the information they need to show the creative teams what they want to see. They guide creative teams as they make their decisions and keep candidates organized so that viable performers don't get lost in the shuffle. In serial television, theme parks, cruise ships, and other mediums, they may be the ones to make the casting decisions outright.

Casting directors are on your side. They want you to be good. Making a good impression and showing them your best work is in your favor. Even if you don't get hired for one project, chances are they will remember you for another down the road. Your relationship should be collaborative but not bothersome. Casting directors should not be expected to manage your career.

## What are self-submissions?

Some casting notices will ask you to submit your picture and resume in consideration for something specific. It is also common for performers to submit an unsolicited picture and resume to a casting office to be put on file for consideration. This is mostly done through regular hardcopy mail, unless a casting notice specifically asks for an email submission. Unsolicited emails may go unopened; however, casting offices always open their hardcopy mail.

Self-submissions should always include a cover letter in which you introduce yourself, ask to be considered for a specific audition or kept in mind for a project, and perhaps speak to your skills as a performer. Cover letters should be short and sweet, but it is important to include the letter with your submission. You cannot expect a casting director to assume what you are after if you don't include a letter stating what it is you want. You should *never* stop by a casting office in person unless invited. You also should refrain from calling a casting office unless they have called you first—and if they do call, listen carefully to the message for pertinent information before calling them back. Once you submit your information, they will contact you if they are interested in seeing you.

In smaller markets, mailing or dropping off a headshot and resume, and a cover letter of introduction, directly to the artistic director of a theater can be enough to get invited to an audition. In Las Vegas, it used to be common practice for dancers and singers to drop their information off to the company manager or dance/line captain of a specific casino show. Though most replacement auditions in Las Vegas are now posted online, there are still some companies that will call performers in for an audition this way.

Self-submitting to production companies who create and manage shows for cruise lines, theme parks, and resorts is still encouraged and could result in being invited to an audition. Even if the audition is an open call, allowing a casting team to know who you are before you walk through the door can help you to be noticed. Check each company's website for self-submission policies.

## Do blind video submissions[27] work?

Blind video submissions can lead to invited auditions. These same production companies for theme parks, cruise ships, and other resort-style entertainment also accept video submissions from dancers and singers. Generally, the producer's website will give specific guidelines as to what they are looking to see on the video. Follow those instructions!

When creating a self-submission video, it is important to include footage in which you are prominently featured and seen and/or heard at your absolute best. Just like any promo reel, you control what the viewer will see. Make sure there is nothing about the video that distracts the viewer from seeing the best of you and your talent. Singing acapella into your webcam or dancing around your living room are *not* the best choices. Rent a studio, put effort into your attire, consider the lighting and camera angle, and give attention to the details. Better yet, use clips of yourself actually in performance if they are available, but choose them wisely. Never ask the viewer to work hard just to find you—using clips of you performing group dances and expecting the casting director to decipher who you are is a quick way to have your video submission tossed out. Though it is not unheard of for performers to be hired directly from a video submission—especially when casting directors need a last-minute replacement—a good video can lead to an invitation to audition in person or a job.

Jodie Stinebaugh is the casting director for Stiletto Entertainment, a Los Angeles-based production company that specializes in live entertainment. They have produced shows for a host of clients, including the five-star cruise ships of Holland America Line and music legend Barry Manilow.

---

[27] Blind submissions: When a performer submits his or her headshot/resume, video, etc. to a casting team without being personally asked to do so.

*It is very rare that I hire a dancer from just a blind video submission. A "live" audition is much preferred. I can better determine abilities like rate of pick-up, execution of details, and matching of stylized choreography. It's very nice to get a feel for a dancer's personality. Video submissions are oftentimes misleading.... I have no idea how dated that work is, nor do I know how long it took him/her to learn and perfect that choreography. In addition, the dancer may no longer look the same. (In this "business of show," I need to ensure "show ready" dancers who are fit and look fantastic in our costumes.)*

## How do I know if a project is "legit?"

This is a common question. We have all heard the nightmare stories, and no one wants to end up like Coco in *Fame*. (If you are unsure of that reference, you might want to put that 1980 film on your watch list!) Knowing whether or not a project is legitimate takes trusting your gut instincts. If something about a job posting strikes you as odd, before you email the company to ask "Is this job for real?", find the answers to these questions:

- ✓ Is it union? It is likely a legitimate job if there is a union attached.
- ✓ What names are attached to the project? If you recognize directors, casting directors, or other actors successful in the industry, that is a good sign. If you don't, Google them and see what comes up.
- ✓ Who is producing? Research the production company and find out the previous legit projects they have produced and how long they have been in business.
- ✓ What does your network know? Reach out to your colleagues to see if anyone knows any information.
- ✓ Where is the audition? Legitimate auditions always take place in studios, theaters, or studio lots. Sometimes they take place in an office or meeting space. They DO NOT take place in someone's private residence. This is especially important to remember when you don't know the person giving the audition—you could find yourself in a dangerous situation over the prospect of a job. The

"casting couch[28]" is not the way you should have to pursue work. You are a professional. Do what you will in your personal life, but true professionals do not conduct business this way.

If you go through this checklist with negative results and the project by an unknown company or an unknown director still sounds too good to be true, I guarantee you it is. It's not real. Move on.

**Is it okay to audition for the same show more than once?**

The answer is always yes, unless you are specifically asked not to. There might be times when a casting team only wants to see people they haven't seen before, but a breakdown will usually tell you that. Otherwise, it can be good to get in front of a casting team multiple times, especially for a long-running show in need of replacements. People who work in casting see hundreds or thousands of performers in a year. Help them remember who you are by showing up, even if you know you are on file. Showing up proves you are interested and eager to put in the work. Often they will cast the person who is freshest in their minds.

Eric Sean Fogel, a professional dancer in opera and musical theater—and now an international choreographer—remembers his audition experience for the 25th Anniversary national tour of *Evita*.

> *They needed a replacement tango dancer so I went to the invited call. It came down to two of us. After the audition they told my agent, "We like Eric for this but are afraid he looks too young. So we are going to hold an open call to see if there is someone a little older." I decided to go to the open call—I didn't shave for a week, let my hair grow out a bit, and showed up with slicked back hair and a mature look. They said, "Eric, you don't have to be here. We like you." But, I stayed through every cut. At the end of the day, they offered me the job. Sometimes you just have to show up and put in some effort in order to prove that you are willing to do the job.*

---

[28] Casting couch: When a director, casting director, producer or other person in charge of casting performers hires (or falsely claims they will hire) a performer in return for sexual favors. Can also be initiated by the performer. This predatory practice is not common but it does exist. Engaging in this behavior is considered unprofessional and is not recommended.

If you were called back for the show before, then they liked your work and you may get called back again. If you were cut before, maybe a track has opened up that you are right for this time. Showing up to audition is part of doing your job as a performer. I once gave a cruise ship audition in Pittsburgh at Point Park University. We were holding multiple open dance calls that day, and I half-jokingly told the 10 a.m. room full of female dancers that if they got cut in the morning they should change their outfit and come back in the afternoon to the next open call and try again. I was going for the laugh, but someone didn't see the humor. It turns out there was a girl we cut in that first round. She went home, pulled her hair up, redid her makeup, changed into a better outfit, and came back in the afternoon. Not only did we keep her through every cut, she ended up booking the job—we didn't even remember her from the morning session… My attempt at humor to ease the audition tension of the room actually motivated her to pull herself together, take a look around at the types we were keeping, and take another stab at it. That time it worked out for her. Incidentally, she waited to tell us these details until well into the rehearsal process for fear we would change our minds. We had a good laugh, but no one ever regretted hiring her!

## How do I know if they are even looking to hire someone at the audition?

One would think that if producers are holding an audition that they are looking to cast the show that day. Many times that is true—many times that is not entirely true. You will encounter instances where roles have been precast or directors and choreographers have stacked the room with performers they already intend to hire. Sometimes the call is a required union call and the creative team isn't even present. The casting director may have sent an intern to sit in the room and go through the motions while the creative team waits to attend the invited calls several weeks later. The producers may be holding a "6 Month Required Call[29]" for a long-running

---

[29] 6 Month Required Call: Part of the agreement that producers and Actors' Equity Association have regarding Broadway and national tours is that an Equity audition will be held twice per year whether or not replacements are actually needed at that time. Casting directors use these calls to build files of performers who may be right down the line once a replacement is needed.

show even though there are no roles actually opening up. For regional theater, there may only be non-union ensemble contracts available even though the producers are holding a union call. From a business perspective, there are a multitude of possible scenarios affecting the producer's intent behind holding the audition.

So, how do you know what the scenario is that day? Unless you can get the inside scoop from someone working on the other side of that table, the answer is you don't—this information is not openly posted for those attending. I am a firm believer, however, that you have to be in the right place at the right time for lightning to strike. It is possible the leading actor they precast could pull out for a bigger offer and leave them in need of a "backup" who fits the part, like you. It is possible that one of the choreographer's favorite dancers could get injured and they need someone like you to take over. It is possible that someone could give their notice to leave a show soon after the 6 Month Required Call and the casting director remembers you from the recent audition. It is possible the casting director might notice you and think of you for another project he or she is casting the next week. Notice a pattern? You have to put yourself out there—it is a part of playing the game. You can't control what you can't control, but you can put yourself in a place for opportunity to happen. That hour out of your day is worth the possibilities.

# THE AUDITION PROCESS

## WHAT TO PREPARE

Auditioning professionally means walking in prepared. Consult the breakdown and make note of any specifics that it calls for. There are a few things you should always have with you at open, invited, or callback auditions.

✓ **Headshot and Resume**: They should be attached back to back with neatly trimmed edges matching perfectly in size. Have a few extra copies with you in your bag/binder in case the casting director requests an additional one. You never know when an extra headshot and resume might come in handy for that other audition down the hall. As always, your headshot should be an accurate representation of you on that particular day for that job.

✓ **Songbook**: You will need this when auditioning for musical theater jobs. Your "book" is a three-ring binder that contains piano sheet music for several song selections in varying styles that you have practiced and prepared with your coach. Include an up-tempo and ballad selections in the styles of traditional musical theater (i.e., Rodgers & Hammerstein), contemporary musical theater (scores from the past 20 or so years), and pop/rock (either from Top 40 radio or a rock-themed score). Your varied selections should feature your legit, belt, and "mixing" vocal techniques and show your range. It may take you some time to build a solid book, and you should work with a vocal coach to create one specific to your abilities and type. There should not be a song in your book that you don't know well—many times a director may ask for a second selection in a different style that you will have to produce on the spot.

  o Your book should contain various cuttings of length, including selections that are 16 bars or 32 bars long and full songs. And, yes, for musical theater auditions even dancers, leads, and character actors need a book with varying options. Make sure any markings like time signatures, key changes, and segues are clearly marked for the accompanist—remember that he or she is sight-reading. Also, don't expect an accompanist to transpose your music into another key. Working with a professional vocal coach or taking an audition class to help you prepare your audition book is worth the investment. For jobs outside the musical theater realm, it isn't a bad idea to have some version of a songbook. You never know when you might be asked to sing for legit theater, video, or television.

o Loose pages of music are not advised—they fall off a piano too easily. A book with a strong binding that can easily close shut "on its own" should be avoided. Copying and arranging the pages of your sheet music in a binder, either in non-glare plastic covers or taped together so they accordion out, will help you prevent mishaps. Some performers are using iPads and tablets in place of a physical book. The jury is still out on this practice—technology is great but is not always fail-proof.

✓ **Prepared Monologues:** Acting auditions for plays will commonly require one or two contrasting prepared monologues. Each monologue should be one to two minutes long. The breakdown, and your own research of the piece, should tell you if they want to see classical or contemporary pieces. Monologues should reflect the same type of character you are auditioning to play. Dancers and musical theater performers are rarely asked for prepared monologues. Having one in your back pocket wouldn't hurt, but it is unlikely you will use it unless auditioning for a non-musical play.

✓ **Sides**: If you were sent sides of a scene to learn, bring the copy with you to refer to. Even if you are memorized (which is not a bad thing!), it is acceptable and wise to have the pages with you in case you need them. Those behind the table generally expect that you will have pages in your hand to prevent stumbling.

✓ **Attire**: Read the audition notice carefully. Know what you are auditioning for and choose the appropriate look. For all auditions,  your clothing choice (and hair styling) will be affected by what you are auditioning for but also the market where you are auditioning. Biggest rule: wear clothing with a line and color that are flattering to your body type and complexion. Trends in audition attire can change—and should be a part of your market research— however, there are some regional differences you should be aware of. The more you learn about the market you are in, the more you will learn about audition attire trends—hone in on it. Learning the preferences of specific directors, casting directors, and choreographers will further affect what you might choose to wear.

As in everything, there is strategy. Above all, make sure you choose the colors, sizes, and lines that show you, your features, and your type at their best.

- o **New York:** For theater auditions, well-fitting and flattering business casual attire is the accepted norm for vocal and most acting auditions. Actors for specific roles may want to wear something that gives a sense of the part without looking costumed. For dance calls, women in leotards and tights and men in jazz/yoga pants and tight T-shirts are prevalent for musical theater. Dancers will have a separate business casual or smart outfit to change into if they are asked to stay and sing. Commercials might require you to wear something specific to what is being sold, but your agent will tell you.

- o **Los Angeles:** The trend is to dress the part for which you are auditioning. For actors, this doesn't necessarily mean a costume, but wearing clothing with a style that fits into a specific time period—with the same attention to hair and makeup—can help auditors see how you fit into that world. Commercial dancers in L.A. are known for putting together outfits that reflect their own individual style and character as well as the style of the commercial gig they are auditioning for. It isn't uncommon for performers to drive around with a car trunk full of audition clothing options.

- o **Las Vegas:** Performers wear more revealing attire in accordance to the style of entertainment. Female dancers opt for fishnets and two-piece dancewear. Men wear clothes that show their physique. Expect to dance in heels.

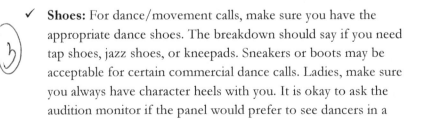

✓ **Shoes:** For dance/movement calls, make sure you have the appropriate dance shoes. The breakdown should say if you need tap shoes, jazz shoes, or kneepads. Sneakers or boots may be acceptable for certain commercial dance calls. Ladies, make sure you always have character heels with you. It is okay to ask the audition monitor if the panel would prefer to see dancers in a certain style of shoe if that information was not posted in the audition notice. And dancers, take note: unless you are auditioning for a modern or contemporary dance company, assuming that you will be allowed to dance barefoot or in socks at an audition is a *huge* mistake. You are entering pet peeve territory. Performers in the show wear shoes. If the excuse is you "can't dance" while wearing shoes, then you are not ready to be a professional dancer....

✓ **Water and Snacks**: Audition days can turn into long days before you know it. You may not have a break to leave the studio and grab something, so have these things in your bag.

## THE SEQUENCE OF EVENTS

Do you wonder what actually happens in a typical professional audition? If you are new to auditioning, this is a legitimate question. There is a basic sequence of events you can expect to encounter at most auditions.

1) **Sign In**: When you arrive at an audition—and you should do your best to arrive early—the first thing you do is sign in with the monitor. At an invited call, they will mark your name as present. At a union call, they will give you an audition card to fill out with your number on it (AEA/AGVA Chorus Call) or a specific time in which to return (Equity Principal Audition). At an open call, they will take down your name and assign you a number, sometimes printed on a sticker for you to wear. There may also be some paperwork to fill out. Monitors will collect pictures and resumes that you can assume will not be returned, even if you are cut from the audition.

2) **Prepare:** After you sign in and if you have arrived early, you will have time to change clothes, stretch out, review your sides, or just find your focus before giving your audition. During this time, monitors or casting directors may also pass out sides, give instructions as to how many bars of a song to sing or style of monologue to give, or what shoes to wear. Every person's pre-audition ritual is different, but use your time to focus on your work

and not your urges to socialize. Respect that even your friends need this preparation time too.

> o An additional note—be respectful of the space you are in. Don't plop your bag down on someone else's. Don't set your coffee down where it will spill on someone's coat. Holding rooms can be crowded, but they are shared space. No one likes the loud, schmoozy, obnoxious jerk when they are trying to get in the zone, so keep it toned down!

3) **Type-Outs**: In the event that a project is seeking only very specific types but a large number of performers show up to an open audition, the casting director or panel has the option to "type out" or release those who don't fit this correct mold. Type-outs don't happen often, but they do happen enough to mention it. Opinions on them vary—some performers believe they should be seen regardless of type while others are happy to not have time wasted if they won't be seriously considered for a project. Both arguments are valid, but ultimately the decision to institute a type-out is beyond a performer's control, and casting people have different reasons for doing it.

4) **Into the Room**: Depending on your number, you may be called into the room in groups to learn a dance combination, or lined up outside before going in alone to sing, give your monologue, or read your side. In a dance audition, you will learn the choreography and then perform it in small groups in front of the panel. For a vocal audition, you will enter the room one at a time, and give your music to the accompanist and discuss cuts, key changes, and tempo. Then, you'll introduce yourself, nod to the accompanist that you are ready, and perform your song. If giving a monologue, you will enter, introduce yourself, and perform your piece or pieces. In a commercial or film audition, you will slate in on camera and then deliver your sides opposite a reader in the room, if required. Taking classes on the art of performance in an audition will help you in this process—these classes are *highly encouraged*. After performing, the auditor panel may give you notes to incorporate and ask you to perform again, or ask for additional

material. Or they may just say "thank you." As one person is exiting the room, the next performer is generally entering unless told otherwise by the casting director.

5) **First Cut**: Sometimes you will be done for the day, and other times the casting director will inform those auditioning who needs to stay for a callback. A callback may consist of learning a new dance combination or performing the first one again, singing a song, learning new sides, showing off tricks, or any other thing necessary to the project. After this round, the panel may make cut further or everyone will be done for the day.

6) **Callback**: Offers might be made immediately; however, most times a callback on a different day is scheduled so that creative teams can see all of the people called back from previous audition rounds. You will again dance combinations, sing songs, read with new scene partners, screen test, or jump through any number of hoops! The casting director may inform you of this immediately following your initial audition or you may receive a phone call or email about the return date. For big jobs, there may be multiple rounds of callbacks on different days. Performers are usually informed the same day if being called back.

7) **The Phone Call:** You may not always be told immediately following the audition when receiving an offer. Most times you will not be told at all if you are out of contention for a job. Everyone waits for "the phone call" to find out if they will be hired. It could take days or weeks. Sometimes it may take six months. This "not knowing" process can be nerve-wracking. Generally, if you hear through your network that the offers have gone out for a job and you haven't been contacted, it is safe to bet that you were passed over. Casting directors do keep extensive records in the event someone turns an offer down or pulls out. Your phone might eventually ring to replace them, but in the meantime don't wait by it. Move on. Live your life. Concentrate on the next audition and leave the last one in the room or you'll drive yourself crazy.

# A HEALTHY APPROACH

**Your audition starts before your work is ever seen.**

Many green performers assume that their audition begins when they walk in the room and are considered only during their time in front of the panel. That assumption is wrong—professionals know that the process begins from the moment they get out of the car or walk up the block. Who is parked next to you? Who is standing beside you in the elevator? Just like your first grade teacher surprisingly didn't live at the school, the panel you are going to be in front of does not only exist in the rehearsal studio. You can only make a first impression once. Eyes and ears are always open, and any witness of rudeness, attitude, complaints, unpreparedness, or general unprofessionalism will surely get back to those making casting decisions. Directors ask monitors questions. Casting directors get information from their assistants. Accompanists are people too and are asked for their opinions, so by all means don't snap at them, either with your tongue or your fingers—treating an accompanist like a "hired hand" says a lot about you as a person. Negative energy can be easily felt, and people steer clear of it.

I was once casting a casino production in Atlantic City. While waiting for the hotel to open the showroom for the audition, I was changing clothes in the bathroom and overheard two male dancers discussing my show they were there to audition for. In the changing room I looked like just another unassuming dancer, but I sure listened to them complain openly about the posted salary, question the content of the show, and trade all the gossip they had heard. All of their energy was negative. I quietly changed and left to go set up the audition. Those two dancers sure were surprised when they walked in the room and found me behind the table ready to teach the combo. They had falsely assumed I was another dancer there to audition for the job. What shouldn't have surprised them is that I had no interest in casting them. Frankly, they weren't really my type of professionals....

**You are there to solve the problem.**

I once had a wise acting teacher describe auditioning to us this way:

the creative team behind the table has a problem—they need to find an actor (or performer) to fit a role. They are hoping the answer to their problem will be you when you walk through the door. Do your best to walk in and solve their problem for them.

It sounds simplistic, but it stuck with me and informed the way I walked into many auditions as a performer. Of course, there is a lot of work involved, but the positive and willing attitude you bring into the room can make all the difference. Wayne Bryan, the producing artistic director of Music Theatre Wichita—who first discovered the young talents of Kelli O'Hara, Kristin Chenoweth, and countless other working professionals—put it this way:

> *Obviously, we behind the table are there because we have an opportunity for someone, and we're hoping to find exactly the right person—the one who will somehow convey, "Trust me; I know what to do with this material. I AM the solution to your casting dilemma." It's a cliché, but actors can never hear too often the truth that the auditors WANT you to be good. They're not sitting there to ridicule or pass judgment. We want to find the talented professionals who will bring some joy into the room and make us want to get to know them better. My biggest dilemma in hiring is the simple fact that I cannot hire all the talented people with whom I come in contact.*

When you are performing in a show, directors and designers call the creative shots. When you first walk into an audition, the opposite is true. Embrace the joy that comes with having the creative control over your own acting choices, song, and wardrobe. In an audition, you are in the spotlight center stage. Own your time in the room—it's yours. Regardless of whether or not you book the job, you can choose to turn auditioning into a positive artistic experience for yourself. Broadway director Philip Wm. McKinley, who helmed *The Boy From Oz* and *Spiderman: Turn Off the Dark* on Broadway as well as international tours of arena spectacles, says performers must remember that an audition is a performance.

> *The basic thing you are doing in an audition is you are entertaining. I just want to be entertained. I want someone to walk in the room and entertain me. Have a good time—I look for that. If we are going to be together eight hours a day over several weeks, I want to know you are going to be enjoyable to hang out with. I think that's important, and a lot of people auditioning forget that.*

## Getting a callback.

Callbacks are never a guarantee you'll be cast, but they are great things. If you made it past the first cut, you can be sure that: a) you are the right type for the project or at least interesting enough that you are still being considered against type, and b) that you did your job as a performer, came in prepared, and delivered a quality performance that grabbed the interest of the creative team, leaving them wanting to see more.

When you come in for your callback, assume that the creative team enjoyed what you did previously. A callback is your chance to remind them of why they liked you and impress them some more. Some people will choose to wear the same clothing they wore to the initial call so they are more recognizable. This is not required but may work to your advantage with certain directors. What you should *not* do is make a large, bold choice in your callback that is exactly the opposite of what you showed originally—unless you are asked by the creative team to do so. A casting director will always inform you of any of these requested alterations. Don't come to the callback with your hair dyed a different color. Don't come in and sing a different style of song unless asked or specifically advised. Do come in prepared, do your best in the room, and know the rest is left up to fate and circumstance. You got called back because they liked you.

# <u>REJECTION</u>

Jay Russell, a New York actor who has appeared in television and Broadway plays, happened to be working in the room during one fateful day of New York callbacks.

> *I was a reader when I first moved to New York for the [1987] Broadway revival of Anything Goes at Lincoln Center. They were casting replacements for the leads and Nathan Lane came in for the role of "Sir Evelyn." At the time, he was far from being famous or known the way he is now. He gave an incredible audition and when he left, Jerry Zaks, the director, said to the room,*

*"Well, this guy has been auditioning for me for 10 years and I've always loved him but have never cast him. Now, finally I want to offer him this role. He was amazing!" The room agreed, but then the casting director said, "Jerry, we still have one more guy we have to see tomorrow before we make any offers, Walter Bobbie. We'll give it to Nathan but let's see Walter first." Well, as we all know, Walter Bobbie ended up being cast in the role and they turned down Nathan Lane.*

This is a great example of not only the ebb and flow of a casting process, but also a director loving the work of one brilliant actor even though that actor was not his final choice. Both actors had talent; only one could get the job. The decision was not personal. This one audition did not break the career of the actor who was passed over. Nathan Lane went on to become a household name as an actor. Walter Bobbie has had a long career as an actor and became a Broadway director, creating the long-running revival of *Chicago*.

The Bureau of Labor Statistics predicts that the number of job opportunities for performing artists will increase as we continue toward the year 2020. They also predict that there will continue to be more qualified performers in the market than there are actual jobs available. The competition is huge, especially in the larger cities where the work happens to be. The odds for everyone, regardless of talent, are that you will book only a fraction of the jobs you audition or submit yourself for. As a professional performer, you will hear "thank you very much" a majority of the time, especially in the early years. Hearing the word "no" just plain sucks. But that's the reality. For some people, the hurt from rejection proves too much, prompting them to leave the business quickly. Those who have the strength to continue pursuing a professional career develop a thick skin and a way to cope. Learning to deal with and process rejection is a skill. Acquiring this skill is different for everyone, but there are ways of thinking which will help you in your process.

- **Getting cut can hurt, but the world won't end.** The process of casting a show is not an exact science. Creative teams have to trust their guts when they make a choice. Getting cut does not mean they didn't like you and it doesn't mean you aren't talented. Do not base your opinion of your talent on the ratio of times you get cut.

Everyone gets cut. Keep working hard, and concentrate on your next audition. You must move on.

- **Do not take it personally!** Getting cut from an audition is not a judgment against you as a human being or your artistic value. You never know exactly what the creative team is looking for or what is going to spark their attention on any given day. If you gave your best, don't worry about "why" you were cut. They may have a certain complexion or height in mind or might be searching for a look that fits the brand of the product. The producers might want a name talent[30] to fill the role in order to sell more tickets. The ensemble track[31] you are right for may also have to understudy a lead role you aren't right for. You won't necessarily know these equations when you walk in the door, nor will you be given an explanation if asked to leave. Sometimes you just aren't right. All you can do is show up prepared to give your best.

- **Don't sweat what you can't control**. If you are auditioning to replace someone and you don't fit the costume, then you don't fit the costume. You can't control that. It can be heartbreaking, but in those moments remember it is a business. You did everything right. That was a financial decision. Next time, maybe you will fit the costume!

- **Don't dwell on the negative**. Deal with your disappointment in the moment and then leave it on the floor and go on with life. Mulling it over for days afterward only makes it hurt worse. You have to let it go. A true professional leaves it in the room.

---

[30] Name talent: A performer who has a degree of fame and a name that audiences will recognize. Producers see this as a potential way to sell more tickets.

[31] Track: A track refers not just to a person's role in a show but a literal tracking of where that person goes on stage, when they move, what they say, where they exit, what they change into, what side of the stage they reenter, etc., throughout a show.

- **Deal with each rejection one at a time**. Every job presents a different set of circumstances, and you can't quantify one audition against the next. Let it be about what you are doing to grow your career and the work you did book; not about the many you didn't. Don't stack rejections on top of each other.

- **Have a support system**. Surround yourself with the people and things that bring you support and comfort. These may include your family, yoga, good friends, prayer, meditation, going to class, eating right, taking a nap, going to the gym, etc. Remove yourself from the things and people in your life who bring you down.

- **Have a life.** Remind yourself that this is a business and your job is to put yourself out there again and again. You have to care and do your best during the audition, and then you need to switch it off and go about your regular life. Have hobbies and interests. Spend social times with friends and time with your family. Go visit "home" when you can. Take a vacation. You can't only live for auditions; that way of living will only eat you alive.

# TAKE IT FROM ME: THE PROFESSIONAL'S EXPERIENCE

One bad audition won't ruin a career. Getting cut one day doesn't mean you will be cut the next. Every professional deals with rejection, has a nightmarish audition, or experiences a level of humiliation that can only come with an artist baring his or her soul in a less than fortunate situation. To stay in this game, you've got to learn to pick yourself up, dust yourself off, and start all over again!

## IN REGARDS TO REJECTION

**Kathleen Marshall** (Tony-winner; Broadway: *Nice Work If You Can Get It, Anything Goes, Pajama Game, Wonderful Town,* and 12 others; film: *Once Upon a Mattress, The Music Man, My Week with Marilyn*)

I have a little mantra for myself, which is, "It's always for credit." Every meeting, every audition, and every event, no matter how big or small, is an opportunity to demonstrate that you are talented, professional, enthusiastic, creative, helpful, and present.

**Shanna Vanderwerker** (Broadway: *Wicked, High Fidelity;* First National Tour: *Wicked*)

It took me at least five auditions for *Wicked* on Broadway before I finally booked it. Sometimes it is absolutely crushing when you don't get a job or a callback simply because you "don't look right". I had assisted choreographer, Christopher Gatelli, on many projects before he landed *South Pacific* on Broadway. I got to the end of the auditions but didn't book the show because the director didn't think I looked right for the show. My singing I can work on, my dancing I can change, but my looks? How can I help that? I called my mom, cried it out, picked myself up off the floor, and kept moving forward because that's what you do. When I was a little girl, my dance teacher taught me that I wouldn't always get what I want, no matter how good I am. It's just the way it is.

**Stephen Carrasco** (Broadway: *Kinky Boots, Ghost, Billy Elliot, White Christmas;* First National Tour: *Young Frankenstein, Kinky Boots*)

Believe in yourself and do everything in your power to put your best foot forward. That's 50 percent. The other 50 percent is *completely out of your control.* So learn to let go of it all after you leave the audition. That way if the phone rings, it's a wonderful surprise.

**Constantine Maroulis** (Broadway: *Jekyll & Hyde, The Wedding Singer;* Best Actor Tony nomination for *Rock of Ages;* television: *American Idol, The Bold and The Beautiful;* sold-out concert tours; Disney national commercial campaign)

> If you're not ready to fail most of the time, then figure out something else to do. You have to know that even the best hitter in baseball bats around .300, let's say. That means 70 percent of the time he is failing. You need to be ready for that rejection so you can learn and grow from it.

**Peggy Hickey** (Broadway: *A Gentleman's Guide to Love and Murder;* television: *90210, Hart of Dixie, Hot In Cleveland, General Hospital;* film: *The Brady Bunch*)

> There's always another show. This is not the only show you will ever audition for or be rejected from. Shows are like buses: there's another one along in five minutes. It's not the end of the world. Whatever you're going out for is exciting but there's another one right behind it that's even better. You just have to have faith in that.

## LESSONS LEARNED THE HARD WAY

**Phil LaDuca** (dance shoe designer/creator for Broadway and film; performer on Broadway: *Singin' in the Rain, Brigadoon*)

> I was the original understudy for "Don Lockwood" (the Gene Kelly role) in *Singin' in the Rain* for Twyla Tharp on Broadway covering the incredible performer Don Correia (one of the greatest male Broadway dancers of our time), but I was only with the show for a short time and never went on as "Don" on Broadway. After a year, the First National Tour of the show was going out with the legendary Peter Gennaro (yes, the *West Side Story/Pajama Game* Peter Gennaro!) as director/choreographer. I had been asked to come in and audition for him for the understudy to the lead, not the role itself as they had already cast the lead with the fellow who had replaced me as

understudy on Broadway. Riled, I went to the audition and NAILED it—the tapping, the dancing, the singing, the acting. And when Peter came up to me to congratulate/hire me, I turned him down to his face! I told him that I should have been offered the lead, not the understudy. What a pretentious ungrateful jerk I was! He was furious with me and I don't blame him now. I had wasted his time and turned down a once in a lifetime opportunity to work with a genius because of foolish pride. I erroneously believed that there would be many, many more opportunities like this. How wrong I was. I let an amazing opportunity pass me by because of ego and pride. (Could there be anything more foolish than turning down a great job?)

**Karla Garcia** (television: *Smash, Divas Live, SYTYCD Season 5* finalist; Broadway: *West Side Story;* First National Tour: *The Addams Family, Wicked*)

I decided to attend an open call for a new Broadway show, *Hot Feet,* choreographed by Maurice Hines. I went to the audition and after I danced, Maurice pulled me up front and said out loud in front of everyone, "Girl, you can dance!" Then, he told us that some dancers would be getting phone calls for callbacks later in the week. The day of the callback arrived, and I hadn't heard anything. I was bummed. I double-checked my email and voicemail to see if I had received anything. NOTHING. Later that afternoon, I decided to check an old email account that I didn't normally check. There was an old message from the casting director saying, "I'm trying to get in touch with you for a callback. We called this number, but it might be wrong. Please get in touch." Oh no! The last digit of my phone number and my email address were wrong on my resume. Because of that I missed the callback! I called the casting office immediately. The casting director laughed, "Karla! We've been looking for you. Unfortunately, there are no other callbacks. But...you booked the show. Maurice loved you. Congratulations." Needless to say, I was *very* lucky. Make sure to proofread your resume!

**Barry Pearl** (film: *Grease, My Favorite Martian;* television: *House, ER, CPO Sharkey, Even Stevens, Criminal Minds, General Hospital;* Broadway: *Baby It's You, The Producers, Lenny's Back, Oliver!, Bye Bye Birdie*)

I was auditioning for *Ragtime* for South Bay Civic Light Opera and had always wanted to play the role of "Tata." The pianist wanted to use her own sheet music instead of what I had brought, because it was more legible. I allowed her to do so. Big mistake! In the middle of the song she stopped playing and said, "My music stops here." I was stunned! I looked over at the director, who said to me, "I've seen all that I needed to see." Suffice it to say, I was furious! But there was nothing I could do. I left with my tail between my legs. The bottom line is I should have either not let the pianist use her own music or I should have taken the time to quickly go over it with her beforehand.

**Justin Greer** (Broadway: *Annie, Anything Goes, The Mystery of Edwin Drood, Shrek, The Producers, Seussical, Urban Cowboy, Annie Get Your Gun;* First National Tour: *Shrek, The Producers;* film: *The Producers*)

I showed up for a singing audition for Savion Glover and was asked if I tap (which I do), and if I had shoes with me (which I had). I was then asked (by SAVION GLOVER!!) to "improv" (which I do NOT do). I absolutely froze. I could think of nothing to even try to do, so I literally ran out of the room. It was terrible. But I learned that sometimes the job is just not for you...

**Bruce Kimmel** (film: *The First Nudie Musical, The Faculty;* television: *The Partridge Family;* Grammy-nominated producer)

After having an incredibly successful decade as a TV and film actor throughout the 1970s, the minute the '80s hit everything became a struggle and got harder and harder—I'd turned 30, the business was changing. I got a call to read for the syndicated version of *Too Close for Comfort.* I arrived early, got the sides, which were awful, and went in and read them for the producer, writer, and director. I was ready to leave when one of them said, "Can't you make it funny?" I turned back slowly and said, "Oh, is that my job? Perhaps one of you should make it funny and then I could make it funny. You can't make funny what isn't funny—isn't that funny?" That was basically the end of my acting career, when I realized I couldn't go through that anymore, but maybe someone else could learn something from this.

## A LACK OF PREPARATION

**Jay Russell** (television: *Law & Order, Boardwalk Empire;* Broadway: *End of the Rainbow, The Play What I Wrote;* national tours *Wicked, Beauty and the Beast*)

A young man came in for a summer stock season I was helping to cast and preceded to do a David Mamet monologue that included about every curse word I had ever heard (and some I hadn't). He screamed and moaned and ended the monologue curled up in a ball under the audition table. There was silence. He finished and got himself up to standing, clearly shaken by his own brilliance. The artistic director of the theatre then calmly said, "*Dames at Sea, The Music Man, The Fantasticks, HMS Pinafore.* Which roles were you interested in?" One more example of an actor not doing his homework....

**Anne Horak** (Broadway: *Chicago, White Christmas;* television: *Royal Pains, A Gifted Man, Law & Order SVU;* First National Tour: *Young Frankenstein*)

I was auditioning for a production of *Annie Get Your Gun* and I didn't read the script. I should have because the character I thought I was auditioning for didn't even exist in the show. After the dance portion, I decided to change into a completely different outfit: a cut-off jean skirt and mukluk [Native American] slippers on my feet. It was totally wrong, completely inappropriate, and yet I thought I was being clever and edgy! The casting director called my agent afterwards and asked, "What the HECK was she wearing? She had slippers on!" My agents called me confused and probably somewhat concerned. I ended up getting an offer anyway, but my mukluks have stayed in the back of my closet.

**Angel Reed** (Broadway: *Rock of Ages;* national tour: *Saturday Night Fever;* national commercials: Target, White Castle; television: *That 70s Show, Eve*)

I was living in L.A. and went to the chorus call for the Los Angeles company of *White Christmas* without fully reading the audition notice or knowing about the show. I made it through the first dance cut. Suddenly, the choreographer, Randy Skinner, starts getting ready to teach everyone an advanced tap combo—I had no idea they were looking for tappers. I don't tap, especially not at that level. I had to politely walk across the room, collect my bags, and exit. I felt totally embarrassed. *Everyone* else knew it was a tap call. I learned from the experience. Never again have I gone into a room without being fully prepared for what I am auditioning for.

## SOME VOCAL MISHAPS

**Lauren Molina** (International concert tour: Sarah Brightman; Broadway: *Sweeney Todd, Rock of Ages;* off-Broadway: *Marry Me a Little;* Helen Hayes Award winner)

I always prepare for my auditions, but sometimes nerves can get the better of you. One of my first auditions in New York City was for the Johnny Cash musical *Ring of Fire* and I brought in a new song: "Jolene." I literally sang the first line, and completely forgot the rest. I apologized, went over to look at the music, tried it again two more times, and just locked up. I forgot the lyrics every time. It was so embarrassing. I could feel my face getting hot and my legs shaking. Needless to say, I did not get a callback for that show.

**Richard J. Hinds** (Broadway: *Newsies, Jekyll & Hyde;* First National Tour: *9 To 5, Disney's High School Musical;* off-Broadway: *Here Lies Love*)

I went to a dance call for *Mamma Mia*. After having made the cut, I was asked to sing. I must have really nailed my vocal callback because a couple days later, I got a call asking me to come back in for an immediate Ensemble/"Sky" understudy replacement for Broadway. I was quite shocked but thought, "If they believed in me, why not?" Well, I got the song and it was much too high for me but I decided to give it the good ol' college try. I walked into the room and there must have been ten people sitting behind the table. They were very clearly looking for someone IMMEDIATELY! I thought, "Well, even if I don't nail the song, I will give it to them with my acting." That's when the casting director said, "We actually don't need to see the scene. Just the song." At that moment I knew it was over but I went for it. I think my voice cracked four times, possibly five. I vaguely recall someone actually gasping during one. I looked around when I finished and the casting director asked, "Does anyone need anything else?" I think they were all still in shock from what they had just witnessed and they just shook their heads "no." I walked out of the room and never auditioned for *Mamma Mia* again.

**Nicholas Cunningham** (Broadway: *La Cage aux Folles*, *The Phantom of the Opera;* West End: *Movin' Out*, *La Cage;* international tour: *Matthew Bourne's Swan Lake*, Pet Shop Boys, Bad Boys of Dance; film: *Nine*)

I sang a song for Marvin Hamlisch that he wrote. I started off well. And then, I forgot the words. I stood there and repeated the exact same verse three times in a row. During the third time through my subtext was, "Right, now you're just singing that verse a third time, so now when you walk out of this room you are going to go downstairs and then hurl yourself in front of the first cab you see on 8th Avenue!"

**Roy Lightner** (Lincoln Center: *Lucky to Be Me*, *Babes In Toyland;* Holland America world tour; Ithaca College faculty)

I went in for the *Catch Me If You Can* pre-Broadway workshop. They wanted a high-range song, and the audition was in a small room with one casting person. I had been out the night before and wasn't feeling well. I could feel the tickle in my throat. I knew it wasn't the best day to sing, but I wanted to go. I went in, put my book down, started singing, and when I went up to hit the high note I cracked SO HARD.

I knew everyone outside could hear it. I went to hit the note in the song a second time, and cracked again. I couldn't finish the song. I wanted out of that room. The accompanist was still playing my song when I decided to leave. Not even a "thank you"—I just left. As I was stepping out the door into a crowded hallway the accompanist called out, "Hey, don't you want your book?" My head was down all the way to the street.

## DANCING DISASTERS

**Matt Kiernan** (Broadway: *Hot Feet;* First National Tour: *Mary Poppins, All Shook Up*)

At a final callback day for a first national tour they had men and women together in the room. Partnering time! My girl had never really done this before, but she barreled through. Then the choreographer, who knew me quite well, said, "Ladies, grab his left hand and fan kick AROUND HIS HEAD into his arm." And we all did, except my girl, who kicked straight up between my legs, smacking me in my naughty place! I was down and was not getting back up, so I left the room, thinking they would call me back for the next round after I could compose myself. They didn't call me back in. But they kept her!!!!

**Linda Mugleston** (Broadway: *Cinderella, Anything Goes, Young Frankenstein, Wonderful Town, Nine, Into the Woods, Kiss Me Kate, On the Town;* television: *The Sound of Music Live!*)

I had to do a movement callback for a Broadway show for the part of, as the director put it, a saucy chambermaid. I learned the combination and then tried to be saucy doing it. It was a struggle. I found it hard to be saucy while seeing myself in the mirror trying to be saucy. The director said, "Very good, very good. Now Linda, I want you to really think of being a saucy chambermaid." Okay, I thought that's what I was doing, but okay, I'll try to be "more saucy." I did the combination again. The director said, "Yes, yes, everyone that was good. Now

Linda, I want you to really put yourself out there…really, really think of being that saucy chambermaid." So I did the combo again…."Very good, everyone, please go out in the hall, we will be right with you. Now Linda, next time you do this, I want to you to really go for it, really put yourself out there, really give us a saucy chambermaid." Holy mackerel! I did the combo a couple more times. I think the director really wanted me to be good, but I just wasn't saucy enough for him. I didn't get the job, but I was okay with that. Being saucy is hard work.

**Troy Edward Bowles** (Broadway: *Chitty Chitty Bang Bang, The Pirate Queen, Movin' Out; The Radio City Christmas Spectacular;* First National Tour: *Mary Poppins*; Cedar Lake Contemporary Ballet)

In an audition for *Miss Saigon*, my pants came down at the beginning of a tumbling pass, baring my bare butt in a dance belt for the whole room. It was embarrassing, but I was able to pull my pants back up in the middle of my final back layout. I have actually seen people leave auditions in an ambulance from tumbling passes. When auditions are a part of your life and career, you are bound to have little mishaps.*

**Denny Paschall** (Broadway: *Chicago, Shrek, Beauty and the Beast*)

The worst thing I ever saw was some guy trying to tumble—who clearly couldn't tumble—take out a crowd of dancers and send himself to the hospital. FYI: Don't say you tumble unless you are AMAZING.*

*[NOTE]: It is unknown if Troy and Denny are talking about the same audition, but my guess is this has happened more than once… Be careful!*

## THAT DIDN'T GO THE WAY I THOUGHT IT WOULD

**Liz Pearce** (Broadway *Billy Elliot;* First National Tour: *Little Shop of Horrors, Seussical, Scooby Doo;* West End: *Metropolis*)

I was called in for the off-Broadway production of *Evil Dead the Musical* for the role of the ditzy blonde. We were asked to prepare material with bold choices and to take risks. I created a medley of songs and rewrote the lyrics as if I was literally a horny man-eating zombie slut. At the end, I whipped a sausage out of my pocket and bit the end off. It was ridiculous but funny...or so I thought. In the world's smallest audition room they'd squeezed a piano and a table of three people, with little room for much else. I started big, despite literally being on top of my auditors. As I sang nobody laughed, not once. They simply glared at me. To make matters worse, I was stuck standing at the end with the sausage in my hand and the accompanist commented out loud, "Well, that was career ending." I was pretty humiliated to say the least. Luckily, it was not career ending, and after some retail therapy I was eventually able to laugh at my absurd audition!

**Philip Wm. McKinley** (Broadway: *Spiderman: Turn Off the Dark, The Boy From Oz;* international tour: *Ringling Bros. and Barnum & Bailey Circus, Ben Hur Live*)

I had just moved to N.Y. and my manager insisted I go in as a replacement for Harvey Fierstein in *Torch Song Trilogy.* I walked in, and I don't know why the hell it happened, but as I started the opening monologue that Harvey did I suddenly began mimicking Harvey's voice, that low, gravelly voice. I don't know what possessed me. I had not rehearsed the monologue that way at all. I don't know what happened. I started and thought, "Well now I have to keep going with this." The casting directors sat there with their jaws dropped open in shock. It was horrifyingly god-awful. I walked out. I was embarrassed that I didn't have the guts to turn and say, "I totally screwed that up." I love actors who do that—admit when they totally mess something up. When they do, I don't take that as a bad audition.

**Jamie Torcellini** (television: *ER*, *The Jamie Foxx Show*; Broadway: *Cats*, *Jerome Robbins Broadway*, *Beauty and the Beast*, *Billy Elliot*)

I once had a casting director follow me out of the audition room to apologize for the director because the director actually got up and stood facing the corner of the room during my audition. The casting director explained that they had just had a fight before I had entered the room. It was odd. That casting director was fired the next day. It's important to remember there are things that are out of your control. Don't take it personally.

## I THINK PERHAPS I MISHEARD YOU

**Ellyn Marie Marsh** (Broadway: *Kinky Boots*, *Priscilla Queen of the Desert*, *Cry Baby*, *Enron*)

My agent told me I was auditioning for "Little Sally" in *Urinetown*. If you know the show, you know it's very stylized and would require a "certain kind" of audition. I went in looking like crap and sang "I'm So Excited" by the Pointer Sisters but played totally pissed, over it and annoyed. It was hilarious!! The casting people were dying. I was feeling good. Then they paused, and then said, "THAT was hilarious, Ellyn. Thank you so much. But this audition is for *The Sound of Music*. We think you might be confused." I made myself into a ball on the ground.... Though it was funny, it was mortifying too. I ran into the casting director a few years later and he told me he has retold that story so many times. Still mortifying.

**William Ryall** (Broadway: *Chaplin*, *Anything Goes*, *Guys & Dolls*, *How the Grinch Stole Christmas*, *Chitty Chitty Bang Bang*, *Seussical*, *Amadeus*, *High Society*, *H2$*, *Best Little Whorehouse Goes Public*, *Grand Hotel*, *Me and My Girl*)

Many years ago I was auditioning for the chorus of the Broadway revival of *Mame* starring Angela Lansbury. This was back in the day when auditions were still held on Broadway stages, a rare occurrence today. I had survived the first two auditions and was called back for the final day. After doing the two dances we had been taught, and singing my 16 bars, we were all told to come on to the stage. (I would guess there was 30 to 40 of us at this point.) As the names were announced I was thrilled to hear "Bill" as part of the list. We were asked to form a line at the front of the stage and anyone whose name had not been called was thanked and dismissed. I was standing center stage in this lineup of very happy actor-singer-dancers as we were told when rehearsals would begin and that Miss Lansbury would be coming to meet her new company in just a few moments. It was then that I noticed one of the casting assistants whispering to the casting director and watched as they carefully counted the number of people in this final lineup. They then said it appeared we had one too many people in the lineup and proceeded to call everyone's name once again—this time using first and last names. When I realized that the "Bill" they called was not me, I waited until they finished the reading of the list and then sheepishly had to raise my hand to say "Excuse me, I think it is me." I remember the walk from center stage to the wings as being one of the most embarrassing moments of my life. I know the casting director was apologizing as I walked but I think the blush of my face had plugged my ears. As I exited the theatre and began my walk home in a stunned stupor, I crossed Eighth Avenue and casually glanced into a cab standing in traffic. Yes, there in the cab sitting as regal as the star she is was Angela Lansbury on her way to the theatre to meet her new company. I think this may have been the first, but certainly not the last, time I cried on the streets of New York.

**Mark Chmiel** (Broadway: *Damn Yankees, Anything Goes*/Lincoln Center)

Years ago, I had a commercial audition for Hallmark Halloween cards. My agent's instructions were, "They want you to come in full Halloween costume." Now, because holiday ads need a bit of lead time in order to be cast, filmed, edited, and aired, the audition was on an extremely hot day…in July. With Halloween months away, I pulled together a popular movie-inspired hybrid look and the next day, hopped on the subway dressed as DAWN OF THE DEAD NERDS. If you are picturing a grown man, in pale ghoulish makeup, greasy spiked hair, horn-rimmed glasses, blood-stained mouth, white socks and loafers, nametag and pencils in my button-down shirt pocket, you are not far off the mark. I got to the audition, sweaty and self-conscious, only to learn my agent had made a mistake. The commercial was for Valentine's Day....

## WHEN BAD AUDITIONS HAPPEN TO GOOD PEOPLE

**Leslie Stevens** (television: *The Young and The Restless, True Blood, Private Practice, Criminal Minds;* Broadway: *La Cage aux Folles, Victor/Victoria*)

I read for a play at Lincoln Center and it felt kind of magical. I was coming to the callback from a coaching across town. Traffic! I was late—they waited for me. I got in there, apologized, managed to breathe and find my connection to the story. It was going great! I took an adjustment and that seemed to be really cool too! Now we were in the postgame chat phase. They were digging me—I was high and over-bubbly on the endorphins of the performance feeling. I walked down next to their table where they had script pages in a pile on the floor. I bunny-squatted down in my longish ingénue dress, put my pages on the pile, and was starting to stand up. Little did I know, my front hem slid under my toes when I squatted, and as I stood up with energy ON—yes, ON—the hem of my skirt, the dress pulled completely taut and LAUNCHED ME like an orca forward and onto my belly with dazzling speed. There was no saving it... SPLAT!! My agent got feedback—"great read but too earthy." Hhhmmmm!? Like gravity-challenged? So much for all that dance training.

**Dante Puleio** (Limón Dance Company; Steps on Broadway faculty)

I was dancing a combination at an audition...badly, very badly! I messed up the beginning, fell out of the turn, was just bad all the way around, and I was not wearing a dance belt. Then, a big développé came in the middle of the combo...and BAM! My pants split all the way open for the whole room to see everything! I got cut. The same thing happened two weeks later at a performance I was doing at an elementary school. Fortunately, I was at least wearing a dance belt that time!

**Gus Kaikkonen** (Broadway: *Equus, The Country Girl;* artistic director of Peterborough Players; playwright; off-Broadway director)

I was seen playing the lead in a play at the 92nd Street Y by a major casting director. The next day she called my agent, was very complimentary, and brought me in to audition for a small role in a Broadway show. It was a classic play and I had already done the part very successfully in the regions—so I knew the sides cold and felt very confident. But I overslept the morning of the audition, jumped out of bed, into my clothes, and rushed to the subway to midtown. In the middle of the audition I felt something odd and put my hand on the back pocket of my jeans. There was an enormous lump on my butt. What the hell? It distracted and confused me and I stumbled over what I was doing in a semi-ridiculous way. Not to mention that I was grabbing and squeezing this unfamiliar growth on my backside. The producer turned to the casting director in frustration and said, "Lynn, where do you find these people?" In a state of confusion I left the audition and went to the restroom, where I discovered that the underwear and socks I had taken off the night before were now rolled up in a ball and lodged in the butt of my jeans. Needless to say I did not get the part. The casting director did call me in again 30 years later for something on *Law & Order*—which I got.

**Stephen DeRosa** (television: *Boardwalk Empire, Ugly Betty, Law & Order, Rescue Me;* Broadway: *The Nance, The Man Who Came to Dinner, Hairspray, Henry IV, Into the Woods, Twentieth Century;* First National Tour: *West Side Story*)

When I'm nervous I tend to run off at the mouth instead of shutting up and just listening and being present. It's not so much when I'm doing the actual work in the audition but either before or after. Well, in one instance after I sang and read pretty well, I said to the director,

"I might be a little fat for this role but don't worry, I'm going to go on the ["Skinny Actress" I can't name here] diet! I mean she's anorexic! Eat a cookie already! Am I right??" Well, it turned out that the director was DATING that "Skinny Actress" I can't name here. The whole room was in shock and I couldn't figure out why. I just left and never heard from them again. In another instance I had finished the audition where I read horribly and in my flop sweat decided to say, "I don't think I was very good just now but I'm just happy I got to come in again because I've had the biggest crush on you since I got out of college. I once followed you and your boyfriend around a department store." So, now I was not only a terrible actor but also a crazy stalker. The moral of the story, kids, is on one level "less is more" but on the biggest scale do your best to KEEP YOUR DIGNITY.

**And there is my very own audition disaster that I will never forget....**

**Adam Cates** (Broadway: *A Gentleman's Guide to Love and Murder, Anything Goes;* First National Tour: *Doctor Dolittle;* television: *90210, Live from Lincoln Center*)

I was auditioning for something at Barrington Stage. I cannot remember the show but it was something I was right for. I usually went to dance calls, but for this show there was an Equity chorus call for singers. I thought I would go in, not with my well-rehearsed standard but a new piece to show them that this dancer could legitimately sing. I chose "On the Street Where You Live" from *My Fair Lady*. I had sung it in a high school choir show (five to six years prior). Sure, I knew it. No need to practice with a piano! I still had this one back-pocket, right? I got the sheet music from my roommate, threw it in my book, and headed off to the audition. I went into the room, introduced myself, and signaled that I was ready to start.

When the accompanist began playing, the song was surprisingly in a much higher key than I remembered it. It wasn't so high that I couldn't sort of handle it, but then we got to the climax. "Let the time go by, I—hehehoohaha...." Not only did I miss the top note by a lot, I broke mid-note into uncomfortable laughter at how terrible I sounded in that excruciating moment. I stopped. I stared at a table full of wide, silent eyes and open jaws. I said, "thank you very much" to THEM, turned around, grabbed my book, and busted out of that room before they could even say a word. I basically cut myself. Nice one, Adam! Never again did I audition with a song that I hadn't rehearsed *repeatedly* with a piano. And I never went in for Barrington Stage again.

## Chapter Five

# Professional Protocol On the Job

**You booked a job!** You beat the odds of rejection, the stars aligned, and your hard work and determination have paid off. Congratulations! Getting the offer is just the beginning; the way you conduct yourself from here forward can affect your reputation and future employment. Working on the professional level is not the same as performing with your dance studio, college department, or a community theater. Though many schools do their best to create as professional of an environment as possible, young performers are inevitably still "green" when they first start out. Professional mistakes are made simply because "you didn't know." The only way to truly experience working professionally is to actually work professionally. Learn from the seasoned professionals around you and respect the fact that they probably know more than you do. For the most part, producers, directors, choreographers, and other professionals understand green performers will make some professional mistakes. There is an implied learning curve, but if you study this chapter you can avoid learning some lessons the hard way and come out ahead. I'm sure one day you'll thank me!

## BEFORE REHEARSAL BEGINS

### ANSWER THE CALL

If a producer wants to hire you, he or she, or their casting director, will call or email you with an offer. Communication is key in any business relationship. Make sure to respond as soon as possible, acknowledge your interest, and thank the person for the offer. You don't have to say yes to everything in the offer right in the moment—taking time to look and think things over with interest is completely acceptable. Just make sure you don't sit on it without giving a response for too long. Unless they request a speedy turnaround, one to three days at most are okay. More than one week is generally too long and communicates disinterest or lack of organization.

If you receive an offer and wish to decline it, make sure you call or email to let the person making the offer know that you cannot accept. You may choose whether or not to tell them specifically why. You would be surprised how often performers just never bother to answer an offer. If you are unable to accept the offer, it is courteous to allow the producer ample time to move on to their next choice. Remember that the person offering you the job has a network too and may share the fact you stood them up. Don't damage your reputation and put possibilities of future work at stake for a silly reason—make sure you always let the employer know as soon as possible whether you accept, have interest in negotiating, or wish to decline an offer.

## CONTRACTS

The details of a producer's employment offer, once agreed to by both parties, will be confirmed with a legally binding written contract.[32] When a casting director or producer calls you with an offer, it is okay to discuss the terms of the offer before you agree to sign the contract. If you have an agent or manager, they deal with contract negotiations for you. If you don't have a representative, you must act as your own, and your response to an offer will be your first interaction with management. These people were not necessarily present at your audition, making this exchange their first impression of you. Put your best foot forward—remember that negotiating a contract doesn't mean you have to hunker down in attack mode. It also doesn't mean the "other side" is out to get you. But it is a chance for you to

---

[32] Contract: The legally binding document that you sign in agreement with a producer that outlines everything that will be expected of both parties while working.

get all necessary information in writing so that you are protected during your employment. Here are some things you should know about your contract before you agree to sign it:

- ✓ **Dates of Commitment**: When are the first rehearsal and the first and last performances? What are the days off? How many hours will you rehearse each day? How many shows per week will you perform? Are all rehearsals and performances in the same city? Is there an option for the contract to extend? Knowing the dates and times (and location) you are committing to are important details. If you are not available for the entire length of the contract, if you need to request a couple specific days off to be in a wedding, if you are ending another job and need to join rehearsals two days late, etc., these are all things that need to be put on the table immediately. Always be honest about the existence of conflicting dates. If a producer or choreographer can work around conflicts, they probably will. If they can't, then they can't. You should always ask up front. If they say no, you may need to rearrange your life on the other end or make sacrifices to accommodate the job you desire. Or you may need to decline the offer altogether. Conflicts can be a determining factor over whether you take a job or not, or whether or not you get an offer in the first place. Being up front about it is a sign of respect for all parties. Lying about it and "calling in sick" on the day of the conflict is not a good plan. (I've seen that happen—it didn't turn out well for that particular actress...)

- ✓ **Union Affiliation**: Usually this is something you would find out for the audition. If it is a union contract, there will be salary minimums and other working conditions that are pre-negotiated. It's good to know what those are, and members can find them on the union's website. Sometimes you can receive a higher rate than the minimum, but often producers institute a "favored nations[33]"

---

[33] Favored nations: This "no-negotiating" tool can be used by producers in both union and non-union contracts. If the job is union, make sure that the favored nations status is written into a rider (an additional page tacked onto the union contract). That way, when the union is reviewing contracts, they can double check that you are in fact being paid the same rate as everyone else.

provision, meaning everyone on that contract will be making the same pre-negotiated rate. If you are non-union and are being offered a union contract, you are allowed to then join the union. Some contracts will require you to join; others will let you pass if you wish not to join. Ask the person offering the contract or call the union to find out. If you are being offered a non-union position with a union production, ask if you can earn EMC points or a SAG voucher, or if you can be upgraded to receive your membership at the end of the contract provided you feel ready to join.

✓ **Salary:** Obviously you want to know how much you are getting paid. Everyone would always love to make more, and it's acceptable to ask for a higher specific wage if you feel the need to. They might say "no." Some theaters simply do not have the budget to offer a performer more money. Some companies have a "favored nations" clause for salaries even in non-union situations. If they do say no to a higher wage, you have to decide if the job is worth the money they offered. At times we all take jobs that don't pay a lot because we just really want to work with a certain director or do a particular show, etc. That's okay. Many times the jobs offered to new professionals are not high paying. Rate of pay is not a reflection of your talent. Expect lower pay rates for non-union jobs early in your career. Additionally, some non-union contracts may offer you one rate for performance weeks and a lower rate for rehearsal weeks. It is not uncommon—don't let it surprise you.

✓ **Travel/Housing:** With only a couple exceptions, union jobs will cover travel to the city or cities where you will rehearse/perform if outside of the city where you auditioned. They will provide housing and local transportation while you are there or per diem to cover expenses. Some long-running resident shows may offer you a relocation package to get you there and get you started; however, you will thereafter be considered a local. These things are not always true of non-union jobs. You need to ask. If they don't cover travel/housing, is the contract long enough and does it pay well enough for you to justify picking up those costs yourself? If it is a non-paying internship, do you have the savings or means to support yourself during the contract period? Will you be required to share a room or house with other cast members? If you informed the casting director or creative team at the audition that you had "local housing", even if you don't technically live in the city of employment but have someone to stay with, then you most likely won't be offered travel or housing or you may only be offered travel for that contract (this can be the case with a union contract as well).

✓ **"Out" Clause**: No one should go into a contract with an intention to quit partway through, but sometimes life happens (personal issues, a higher-paying gig, etc.) and you need to know what your options are. Should you need to terminate your employment mid-contract, are there stipulations? In a union contract, a two- or four-week notice is pre-negotiated, as are reasons for leaving and severance. For a non-union contract, find out if you can give notice or if there is absolutely no way to get out of the contract. Find out if you will also be required to pay for the costs of hiring and training your replacement and what those are—some producers do ask this, so don't let it surprise you. Also, on the flip side, does the contract provide for you in any way should the producer terminate your contract early? Will you receive a severance? All of these talking points should be a part of your written contract.

✓ **Additional Duties**: Are you being asked to understudy, swing, dance captain, or perform an additional technical assignment? Will you be required to perform additional work duties besides those directly related to performing; i.e., on a ship (activities staff), in a theme park (meet and greet in character or parade escort), or at a dinner theater (wait staff)? On union contracts, additional payments for extra duties (called "bump-ups") are at pre-determined rates. If the contract is non-union, will you receive an additional fee for these extra duties? If they are unable to offer additional money, you need to decide if it is still worth it for you to take the job with these additional duties for the amount of money offered. The producer may move on to another performer if you turn additional duties down. If you insist on no duties, be prepared to be passed over. You must make the decision that will make you happiest even if it means compromising or working more hours.

✓ **Specifics for Film and TV**: It is rare that someone books a role in film or TV without representation to handle contract negotiations; however, some specific topics you will need to know about your contract include: the minimum number of work days/weeks/episodes that are guaranteed (at times the dates may not be sequential), set accommodations (keep in mind you will be spending a lot of time in your dressing room/trailer), wardrobe (for smaller-budget work you may be asked to provide your own wardrobe for a rental fee; if wardrobe is provided, you may have an option to purchase it at a discount), and copy/credit (being provided a copy of your work for your own promotional use and what your billing will be in the credits).

When you are negotiating your own contracts, it is okay to ask for what you want. You might not get what you want, but remember it is all business—don't take it personally. The worst response someone can give you is "no." There is no harm in asking, but there is a difference between negotiating politely and making demands. Tone is always something to be mindful of. You can stand up for your needs while still being respectful of other professionals. Don't go into your negotiations with the attitude that management is the enemy. If performers feel happy and taken care of, the outcome is better for everyone. Management understands that. Remember to stay polite. Remain non-emotional. That is not the same thing as rolling over. If an employer is not able to offer something you want, weigh its importance to you. Is that one line item really so important that it's worth declining the entire contract? If it *is*, that's ok as long as you are making a strong/wise business decision and not throwing a tantrum.

If a producer offers you professional work, but refuses to enter into a professional, legal contract, it should raise a red flag. It doesn't necessarily mean the job is not legitimate (a majority of the professional work you do *will* involve a signed contract), but it does mean you need to do your research in depth before you commit. Contracts are designed to protect the interests of *both* parties. Working without a contract means producers are not limited in what they can ask of you and you have limited protection against professional abuse. At the same time, there is nothing to stop you from walking out and leaving a production in the lurch. The bottom line is, if you can get a signed contract you should get a signed contract. There will be fewer surprises for everyone that way.

## What is a "Plus 10"?

"Plus 10" is a term you may have heard, and it only applies to contract negotiations when you have representation. If you have an agent to negotiate your contracts, there are times when he or she can get a producer to pay a "Plus 10." This provision means the producer will cover the agent's 10% commission fee out of the producer's pocket instead of your own.

## ARTISTIC PREPARATION

You will likely be sent a script or music before the first rehearsal. If the creative team wants you to have the material prior, then it is safe to assume they also want you to be more than familiar with it. If you have spoken lines, plan to memorize them before you walk in the door to rehearse a specific scene. If you will be singing, learn the songs and lyrics if not your actual vocal part for harmonies. Obviously you won't be able to learn the choreography before you get there, but go to dance classes and the gym regularly to be in the best dance shape possible when you arrive for work. Do your own research about the story, time period, and characters to come in with knowledge and an ability to contribute to discussions and character interpretation. If it's a revival, find out about the history of the piece. Above all, don't wait until day one of rehearsal to crack open the book....

## FITTINGS

You could be asked to come in for a costume or shoe fitting or to send in your physical measurements well before rehearsal begins. This is extremely important—time is money. The entire timeline for the wardrobe department will depend upon your attention to this. For a fitting, make sure you bring appropriate dance undergarments and dance shoes so that things can be altered properly. When you try on a costume that you know you will have to dance in, test your range of motion to see if you will be able to accomplish whatever the choreographer asks while wearing the clothes. If you know you will be doing partnering or tumbling, make sure that the clothes allow you to fully extend your arms over your head. The wardrobe team isn't in the rehearsal room with you. Providing them the information they need regarding the functionality will allow you to do your job better down the line. Above all, be kind and respectful to the wardrobe team. Keep in mind that you are not hired for your artistic opinion concerning the clothes; you are hired for your performance. You may not like a costume design, but it is someone else's artistic work (and he or she will likely be in the room with you). Mind your manners. You wouldn't appreciate a costume designer telling you that they didn't like your performance, so extend the same courtesy.

# THE FIRST DAY OF SCHOOL

*The most important thing for anyone to bring into the audition room or the rehearsal room is focus and energy. If you don't bring that, I'm not sure why you're there.*

**-Kathleen Marshall, award-winning director/choreographer**

The first day of rehearsal for a professional job is exciting. The energy will be infectious. You will be meeting your fellow performers and sometimes the creative team for the first time. As in any professional business setting, there is an unspoken protocol that is expected from day one: Keep on top of your game.

## WHAT TO BRING

Be prepared on the first day so that you can be your best professional self. Here's a checklist of what you'll need to pack in your bag:

- ✓ Any materials that were sent to you previously: script, musical score, etc., and a pencil!

- ✓ A refillable water bottle. You'll want it.

✓ A voice recorder, pencil, and your score if you are being asked to learn music. In music rehearsals, you should record your part so that you have it to practice later, especially if you do not read music. Singers will know to do this. Dancers or actors who are new to singing might not. Having that recording to refer back to will help you review correctly.

✓ Your own appropriate rehearsal shoes. Dance heels, character shoes, jazz shoes, jazz sneakers, appropriate athletic sneakers, or perhaps tap or pointe shoes should be in your bag. Socks or foot thongs are not appropriate unless the choreographer specifically tells you they are. Be smart—find out the choreographer's preferences. For non-dancing roles, comfortable but supportive footwear is preferable. Ladies may bring heels if they are appropriate to the character and give your ankles stability. UGGs, open-toed sandals, or trendy shoes with no ankle support are not appropriate. Flip- flops are just dangerous. Working barefoot is completely unacceptable unless you are doing specific choreography or playing a scene that calls for it and stage management has made the room safe for that purpose. As time progresses, you will eventually have the opportunity to wear your "show shoes" while in rehearsal so you can slowly break them in.

Make sure the rehearsal clothing you wear is something that allows the creative team to see your line and won't inhibit movement. It is okay to wear clothing that moves a specific way if you are acting in a period piece (jackets, rehearsal skirts, etc.) or helps you to feel in character—the wardrobe department might have items you can wear. Whatever you wear to rehearsal, make sure it is clean.

Don't be gross—take a shower, do your hair, wear deodorant, brush your teeth, use breath mints, etc. Personal hygiene is important when you are working in close proximity with others—don't overlook this, even if you don't find these things to be important in your own daily life. Some of your colleagues may be highly sensitive or allergic to certain perfumes or colognes, so abstain from wearing them. If you smoke, avoid smelling like an ashtray. (And think about quitting…)

# WHO'S WHO

In addition to your fellow performers, there will also be people with specific job titles in the room. Learning who they are and what they do will allow you to know whom to go to with appropriate issues. Going through proper channels of communication is a way to keep from stepping on toes. You should already know what the director and choreographer do (if you don't, please refer back to Chapter 1: Training!), but any of the following could be a part of the rehearsal process.

- **Associate or Assistant Choreographer or Director[34]:** This person is the choreographer or director's right hand. There may be more than one. They usually have an established professional relationship with the person they are assisting and may help them both administratively and artistically. You can go to this person with simple questions about blocking, counts, notes etc., so as not to distract the director or choreographer. If one of them gives you a performance note, consider it as having come directly from the director or choreographer. Today's assistants are tomorrow's directors—establishing a good working relationship is in your favor.

- **Musical Director:** In a musical or show with live music, this person is in charge of teaching the vocal parts to the cast and coordinating with the live musicians (if any), and may even serve as conductor and/or accompanist. He or she is a full collaborator on the creative team and will give notes to performers. This person may also have an assistant or assign a Vocal Captain from within the cast.

- **Dance Captain:** Sometimes called a Line Captain. This person might also be an assistant to the choreographer or just someone else new in the cast learning the show alongside you. He or she will be responsible for maintaining the show once it is open and the choreographer leaves. Dance captains document and learn all choreography and staging for every performer's track. They are

---

[34] Assistant directors: In film, television, and opera they are referred to as "A.D.s"

empowered to give notes to other performers, conduct choreography cleaning sessions, teach and put in replacement and understudy performers, and work with management overall.

- **Resident Supervisor:** Sometimes called a Resident Director. If a show is long running and the director is not often involved, a resident director might be hired to maintain the show artistically. This person auditions and teaches replacement cast members throughout the run. If there are multiple companies of the same show, the resident supervisor is in charge of making sure all the companies match and retain the same quality standards. There are also Resident Choreographers or Music Supervisors who perform similar duties relating to dance or music.

- **Understudy:** This is a performer, usually an ensemble member, who, in addition to his or her own track, learns and can step into a leading or principal role in the event the regular performer is absent.

- **Swing:** This is a performer who learns multiple ensemble tracks and can jump into any one at a moment's notice should the regular performer become ill or need to miss a show. Many times a dance captain will also swing a show, but not always. A swing is different from an understudy. If an understudy has to go on in the principal role he or she is covering, a swing would then go into that person's vacant ensemble track. Sometimes swings also understudy leading and principal roles in addition to covering the ensemble.

- **Standby:** This is a performer whose sole purpose is to step in for the lead should the regular actor need to miss a performance or leave stage partway through a performance. A standby does not perform any other role in the show; thus, they "stand by" in the wings. This is different from an understudy who learns his or her own onstage track while also covering a role.

- **Stage Manager:** This person, also called a PSM (production stage manager), is responsible for making the rehearsal room run smoothly. Along with the ASMs (assistant stage managers), they prep the rehearsal space, document the show, manage the moving of set pieces, keep track of time so everyone gets proper breaks, ensure that performers have the materials and information they need such as scripts and call times, create the daily schedule, and much more. For stage productions working under a union contract, the stage managers also make sure union rules are strictly followed. They are members of the performers unions as well. Once the show opens, the stage manager is responsible for calling all of the technical cues and maintaining the artistic integrity of the show while the ASMs manage the backstage crew. Stage managers are usually the busiest people in the room and are the people you can go to for problem-solving issues that relate to the show or interaction with fellow performers. On film sets, the A.D.s perform many of the same functions as a stage manager in theater.

- **Company Manager:** This position is different from a stage manager. A company manager is responsible for the business side as it relates to the production and not for the artistic quality. Company managers handle human resource issues such as payroll, contracts, housing, and travel among other things. They are the people you go to with any issues beyond those relating directly to your performance.

- **Producer:** This title can mean different things, but generally these are the people who allow a project to happen. There are producers who option rights from writers, hire creative teams, and secure financing. There are producers whose sole job is to secure project financing. There are producers who pitch and are hired to create shows and events for larger corporations. There are executive producers, artistic directors, or managing directors who work for not-for-profit theaters and share responsibilities for all of these things. Ultimately, it is important to know that producers are the people who sign your check!

## FIRST THINGS FIRST

Make the right impression from the time you first walk in the door.

- Don't be late!!!!! There is no worse way to make a bad first impression than to be late. If anything, get there early. A wise teacher once told me, "If you walk in right on time, then you are already 10 minutes late." Time is money in this business; don't disrespect your colleagues by expecting them to wait for you. Plan ahead for traffic. If an emergency arises forcing you to be tardy, call your stage manager immediately.

- Be warmed up and ready to dance or sing by the start time of rehearsal. Ask the stage manager prior to rehearsal if the studio will be available early to physically warm up. If it's not, take the time at home or go to a class prior to rehearsal so that your body is warm and ready to go when rehearsal beings. Some choreographers may offer an open warm-up session as an option. Vocal warm-ups should always be done *before* you arrive.

- Learn everyone's name quickly. This is a learned skill, but it can make a difference in how other people are willing to relate to you. Knowing whom you are working with, even on a short gig, is helpful in building your network.

- Turn the ringer off on your phone. Do I have to explain this one?

## RESPECT THE REHEARSAL PROCESS

Every director will work a little differently, but there are some general rules that you should follow while working in rehearsal and participating in the creative process.

- Listen, listen, listen! In rehearsal, it is important to calm down, pay attention, be quiet, and listen to the director or choreographer. Learn to listen deeply to what is being said so that you don't have to ask a million questions later.

- When you are learning, always dance full, sing full, and act full unless the creative team specifically tells you it is okay to mark[35]. Not only will it help you build the necessary stamina, it will allow the creative team to see what they are creating.

- Pay attention to your spacing and be as consistent as you can. Use the number line[36] or spike marks on the floor to maintain your formations or blocking. You must have a character brain that is fully invested in the movement/story and an actor brain that is aware of elements like spacing and where the audience or cameras are.

- Take the performance notes you are given gracefully. If you need further clarification or problem solving, it is okay to ask, but resist the urge to over-explain why you did something wrong or blame it on another performer. Be conscious to incorporate the given note into the next run-through.

- Don't assume you will just remember the details. Preferably on a break, take time to write down spacing numbers and blocking notes in your script or a notebook. Keep your notes updated with changes so that you always have a record of the current version. You may not come back to a scene or dance number for a few days after you learn it, but you will be expected to recreate the exact details the first time you come back to run it.

- Be patient and collaborative with your dance/scene partners. They rely on you too. It is unfair to wait to find your character or performance until you get to the stage. Work together in rehearsal

---

[35] Mark: To hold back from performing full out in order to conserve physical energy or voice.
[36] Number line: When working in Equity musicals and on most stages, a number line will usually be painted on the downstage edge of the stage. There will be a "0" at the exact center of the stage and then markings usually every two feet that go all the way across to the ends of the playable space. Usually the markings are even numbers indicating how many feet away from center they are. Number lines are also taped out in the rehearsal room to make transfer to the stage easier.

with the direction you are given. Share your ideas. Start playing with choices. Feel free to "act!"

- Choose to be generous—not selfish. Be a team player who looks at the story as a whole. It can't be all about your own moment. Upstaging or pulling focus unnecessarily doesn't serve the piece. Your laugh lines are not more important than your colleagues'. Play nice in the sandbox! Always support the action in a scene with your energy, regardless if you are a lead, supporting, ensemble or background.

- Resist the urge to derail your director or choreographer. Don't try to do their jobs for them. It isn't that your artistic opinions aren't valid (they might actually be better!), but unless you are invited by the director to interject when something isn't working, allow the director to direct. Every director works differently in his or her process, and just because one director wanted all of your ideas, it doesn't mean the next one will. Feel it out before you speak up, especially when working with someone for the first time.

- Be present and open. Be conscious of your attitude and body language while in rehearsal. You might not intend to be communicating negativity by the way you are standing with your hands on your hips, yawning, sighing big or rolling your eyes, but those things can all be taken the wrong way. Uncross your arms and look open even if you're not truly feeling it. No matter how tired you are, don't stare at the director or choreographer like you want to kill them for asking you to do it one more time. They remember things like that....

- Be a "make it work" person. A director or choreographer may ask you to try an intention or a cross or a movement that you don't agree with or don't think will work. Go for it anyway. Try it. Really try it. Don't be the person who sabotages the request just to prove it won't work. If it really isn't meant to be, a good director will try something else. Let them make that call.

- Be open to change. Lengths of a rehearsal process vary per project. Creative teams will make changes throughout the studio process. They will make changes during tech. They will make changes during dress rehearsals and previews. Sometimes they will come back and make changes after the show has been frozen[37] for opening night. You may not like the changes being made, but be patient, try to see the bigger picture, and respect the decisions of the team.

# AT THE END OF THE DAY

Rehearsals can be exhausting days, but be mindful that an artist's workday carries different expectations than a "regular job." There are some things you need to be mindful of when you leave work for the day.

- Do your homework. After a choreographer or director gives you the material, it is your responsibility to know it. Take the necessary time you might need outside of rehearsal to review so that the next time the scene or number is run, you can deliver it proficiently and know what you are doing. Making a mistake and not actually knowing your choreography or staging are two very different things.

- Take care of yourself. Your body is your livelihood and others are investing money in your performance. Everyone in the room is relying on you to stay as healthy as you can.

- Be wary about what you post on social media regarding the daily process. The people you work with and for might not want their lives and work in progress plastered across the Internet. Be respectful.

---

[37] Frozen: When a creative team decides to stop making changes to a production, usually during previews prior to opening night, a show is considered to be "frozen."

# PROTOCOL FOR UNDERSTUDIES, SWINGS, & STANDBYS

When performing in theater and stage productions, you may find yourself being hired for one of these jobs even early on in your career. Being cast as an understudy, swing or standby (also referred to as a "cover," because in the event of someone's absence their track is still "covered") does not mean the creative team feels you are second best or not good enough to play a regular role. In fact, it is just the opposite. It means they trust your talent and skill level enough that you can jump in and save a performance at a moment's notice. Covering roles is an honor—these job titles carry great responsibility.

There is no formal schooling in how to accomplish this job successfully, but there is protocol that will help you should you need to go on. The job of covering begins on day one of rehearsal, though you should also prepare artistically as you would for any other role.

**Take good notes.** If you are an understudy, your first priority should be to learn and execute your regular track. At the same time, pay attention to the blocking and direction being given to the person playing the role you are covering. Make notes on the role in your script in addition to the notes you are making for your own track. Using a different color pencil or highlighter to differentiate roles will prove helpful. When you are not being used in rehearsal, ask the stage manager if you can sit in on rehearsals to observe the person in the role being directed. Learn as much of the role as you can on your own—once the show opens, you will have your own understudy rehearsals to fill in the blanks.

If you are swinging the ensemble or acting as standby for a particular role, you are expected to be present for all rehearsals. Standbys should keep written record of all direction, blocking, tracking, and intention pertaining to the role. The job of the swing is more complicated because you are usually covering multiple roles. Organization is key. You must keep detailed notes on all of the tracks you cover including charts of formations, spacing and traffic. Ask your stage manager if you can have photocopies of the "minis." These are ground plans of the set shrunk down to letter size that are helpful when charting where everyone is on the stage. Once in the theater, observe off-stage patterns for costume changes as well.

There is no codified system for swinging—swings usually come up with their own system that makes sense to them. Most keep a binder or book with organized, color-coded notations. Some create notecards for each track that can easily be concealed in a pocket for quick access. Swings should get up in the back of the room and learn choreography as it is being taught so that it gets into the body. Pay attention to the details and the blocking. If you are cast as a swing, it's not a bad idea to reach out to your network and ask for tips from someone who has done the job before. Good swings have good ideas to share. It is a hard job, but it can be extremely fulfilling.

**Be consistent and restrained.** As you are learning a role, it is okay to explore the ways you can make the role your own. You don't have to impersonate the regular performer, but you must still adhere to the blocking, business, beats, and intentions set by the director. You must execute the same steps and movement styles set by the choreographer. You can work with the musical director to find the nuances of the music that fit well with your voice, but you also must sing everything in the same key as the other actor. Fellow performers will rely on your consistency so they too can execute their roles. While the director and regular performer are in the process of collaborating to create the role, unless you are very specifically invited to do so (which would be rare), it is not the place of the cover to interject thoughts and ideas. Your job is to respectfully observe and notate. Save your questions for the associate director or choreographer, stage manager, or dance captain and find an unobtrusive time to ask. It isn't that no one cares about your needs, but when rehearsal time is short, priority must be given to the person playing the role regularly. Eventually, you will be given the attention. Additionally, suppress the urge to circle the role like a shark. Everyone, including you, was cast in their track for a reason including the person you happen to be understudying. Don't let your eagerness at a chance to play a lead cause an awkward dynamic within the cast. There is a fine line between being ambitious and becoming obnoxious. Creative teams and management notice this.

**Fill in when possible.** Throughout the rehearsal process, there will inevitably be times where a regular performer will be out of the room for a costume fitting or press interview. At the discretion of the director, this gift of opportunity can be a way for you to put the role you are covering on its feet. Be prepared to jump in whenever possible and be as memorized as you can. During rehearsal, most will be patient if you need book-in-hand for part of the time. Be careful of "winging it" when it comes to partnering lifts, combat, or stunts that you have not yet had a chance to learn safely and full out. Safety is first, but this is a helpful way to learn.

**Be ready to go on without a rehearsal.** Once a show opens, the stage manager, and dance captain will conduct weekly rehearsals so that understudies, standbys, and swings get ample stage time and clear direction of the material. But you should do everything to ready yourself to go on well before opening night happens. Once public performances begin, even during the preview period, you could be called to go on at any time even if understudy rehearsals have not yet commenced. It will be expected that you know the material.

As a swing, I have found myself jumping into a track onstage with no put-in rehearsal, executing a role for the very first time in front of a paying preview audience. As an assistant, I have found myself putting in an understudy at half-hour call and tracking them around backstage to remind them of last-minute blocking and line changes before they rushed back out onstage with no proper rehearsal (on Broadway, no less). It happens often! In the event you do have to go on, be rest assured that everyone from the stage managers to wardrobe to the creative team to your fellow cast members will do everything they can to help you to prepare and succeed. But out there on stage, you have to deliver the performance. The audience should never walk away feeling as though they saw a subpar performance because an understudy was on. Know your stuff!

**When you do go on, enjoy!** Performing the role you cover is stressful at first but it is also very exciting. The more prepared you make yourself beforehand, the easier time you will have. Enjoy your moment in the spotlight and give the best performance you can. Modern audiences may groan when they learn an understudy is going on—don't let that discourage you. Show them in the first few moments why you were hired to cover a role. Be the great performer you know you are. I promise you the audience will be won over in no time.

*A note to fellow cast members*: If a swing, standby or understudy does have to go on, a little kindness and understanding on your part will go a long way. The job they are doing is the hardest job in the cast, and being supportive of their efforts will only help the artistic value of the show. They may make some mistakes, go the wrong way, flub a line, etc., but forgive them before those mistakes even happen. Gently help them out on and off stage. We call it "shove with love" (though you shouldn't actually shove them unless they are about to be seriously harmed for being in the wrong spot). Also, if you are playing a role with an assigned understudy, don't let your own insecurities dictate the way you treat that person. Your graciousness will keep your relationship from feeling awkward. Ultimately, you are lucky to have them there. Be kind.

## Chapter Six

# Your Support Staff

Like any other small business, professional performers may engage the services of contractors and become members of professional associations. In this chapter, we will discuss the roles that other professionals and organizations might play in your business as your representative.

## AGENTS

Young performers tend to feel a lot of pressure to secure an agent as soon as possible. There are some teachers who help their students develop impeccable technique and then send them out the door saying if they just sign with an agent their career will take care of itself. That final sentiment is unfortunately misleading. The truth is that some performers go through their entire careers working steadily without ever having had an agent. There are also many advantages to having an agent, depending upon the market you are in, types of roles you hope to book, and the medium you are pursuing. To understand if an agent is right for you, it is important to know what they do and how they can help you.

An agent is a person who specializes in handling some of the business aspects of a performer's career. Your agent helps you with choosing headshots, editing your resume, and defining your look and type. Agents get breakdowns directly from a casting director and submit those clients whom he or she feels may be right for the project. Agents secure interviews or audition appointments. If you book a job, the agent will take care of all contract negotiations and make sure all of your paperwork is done. While on a job, your agent will serve as a liaison between you and the producer should any contract infractions arise. Legitimate agents are licensed by the state and franchised by the unions, which means they have entered into an agreement with the various artist unions guaranteeing they will play by the rules and not take advantage of union clients. You should be cautious of unlicensed "agents."

Agents will make a commission of 10% of your total performance earnings. If you are signed with an agency, you should pay a commission from any professional performance job you book whether they sent you on the initial audition or not. Some performers don't think that seems fair— why should you have to pay an agent when you booked the job from an open call? Your agent is your business partner and is only paid when you book a job. How many auditions has your agent sent you on where you didn't book the job? They weren't paid for their time in those instances, yet they still took time to pitch you. You are both investing in your career and should both be financially rewarded when the payoff comes.

Agents make money through volume—the more clients they have working, the more income they make—and agents are not there to "get you work." You are the one who must get you work. Agents are there to help open doors for you.

## REASONS TO HAVE AN AGENT

Agents can do great things by giving you greater access to opportunity. Agents have relationships with and the trust of casting directors. They can get you audition appointments at the invited calls that you wouldn't otherwise get. They have access to breakdowns that you won't. In New York, L.A., and other markets, having an agent is necessary for the film, television, and commercial industry. Casting notices are sent to agents and are not posted publicly—it will be difficult to get your foot in the door in an industry that only wants to see represented talent. Most commercial dance auditions are exclusive to dance agency submissions. For all of these jobs, especially in the Los Angeles market, an agent can help open doors for you sooner rather than later. On the East Coast, having an agent is helpful in getting you seen for invited Broadway calls, especially as replacements. Actors going in for principal roles in the bigger theaters and tours can benefit from an agent in being seen and negotiating contracts. Opera singers who are dealing in the international market most definitely need one. Agents can also help guide you as your career continues to develop.

## REASONS *NOT* TO HAVE AN AGENT

The necessity of having an agent depends on what market you are in, where you are in your career, what type of work you are pursuing, and what your talent level is. To work steadily in Las Vegas shows, cruise ships, theme parks, resort shows, and regional, stock, dinner, and non-union theater, an agent is not necessary. In New York City, it is possible to become a Broadway performer without one. You can go to open and union-required calls, and sometimes they do cast from those calls. When it comes to regional ensemble work, you can generally be seen at open and Equity calls. If casting directors in musical theater know you, they might call you in regardless of representation, even for Broadway replacements. Concert dancers generally don't need agents unless they also have commercial dealings. You are always allowed to negotiate your own contracts. When contracts are favored-nations minimums, an agent will not be able to negotiate any higher fee than you can.

## WHEN TO GET AN AGENT

For many performers in major markets, there does come a time when an agent can prove to be very helpful. This is different for everyone. Listen to the advice of your mentors in the business, and evaluate your own career honestly. To determine if the time is right for you to seek representation, ask yourself some market and career analysis questions:

- ✓ Does the type of work you want to pursue require someone to submit you (i.e., television/film)?
- ✓ Do the working people around you who match your type/talent have representation, and are they booking jobs primarily through agent-invited calls?
- ✓ Do you have some clear career goals or are you still trying to figure out what you want to do in the industry?
- ✓ Are you getting called in frequently by casting directors for jobs that you want without having an agent?
- ✓ Do you have directors and choreographers who call you in for their auditions and hire you consistently?

✓ Are your skills at a level where you can compete with the next tier of professionals?

✓ Have you been able to book professional work on your own, giving you some credits that show an agent you have potential?

✓ Are you ready to make the commitment and invest in a professional relationship?

Being ready to sign with an agent means you are ready to make a career and life shift. Your day-to-day may require some adjusting—you must be prepared to jump into the fast-paced professional world with both feet. If an agent is going to invest hours of time pitching you, you must be ready and willing to make yourself available for the auditions or interviews they secure for you. You have to be ready to make others aware of your travel schedule. You have to be organized. You have to be 100 percent on top of your game to truly be ready. Getting an agent is not the answer to starting a career—it is a way to help you further the career you have already begun.

## HOW TO GET AN AGENT

This can be pure strategy, and networking comes heavily into play here. The best way to get a meeting toward representation is for an agent's current and trusted client to recommend you. If you have a colleague with whom you have a great working relationship who has an agent whom you are interested in meeting, you might ask if he or she could specifically recommend you. One way to get on the radar is to ask your friend/colleague to arrange a no-pressure introduction with their agent at a social event. The more likely way, however, is to ask that they call their agent and recommend you. When you then submit your information (and you should directly reference your colleague's name in your cover letter), the agent will be on the lookout for you.

Beyond personal recommendations, agents will scout talent by attending performances to find performers who fit into their roster. It is acceptable to send a postcard invitation to an agency of interest if you are performing in a show nearby. Some agents will attend showcases and classes to look for new talent or hold open and union-required auditions when they are looking to build their client files. And, of course, taking audition classes taught by knowledgeable agents is another way to meet face to face and have your talent seen.

People do send blind mail submissions to agencies. These might lead to meetings if the timing is right, but they are the least common way to secure representation. When mailing a new submission to an agency, you should include your picture and resume as well as a short cover letter that introduces you, your career goals, and your intent in seeking representation. You might also include your reel. Be sure to look at an agency's website to find out their preferences for new submissions and learn more about the specific types of talent they represent.

## What kind of agent should I get?

Just as performers tend to have specialties in skill and talent, agencies tend to specialize in representing talent for specific aspects of the industry. Some agencies only deal in commercials and advertising or voiceover artists. Some handle dancers and choreographers, or opera singers, or legit film/theater actors, or children, or major stars. There are boutique agencies that may only represent a limited number of clients, and large agencies with offices in several cities that represent a broader spectrum of talent. There are agents who only represent a handful of clients who all differ in type in order to focus their submissions. Other agencies represent many performers of the same type and submit all of those people for a limited number of audition slots.

Personality type can come into play. Agents are people too! Some are intense and some are unobtrusive. Finding the type of agency and agent who is right for you is part of the equation. You must do your research to find those agencies with which you feel you, your type, your work method, and your skill set would be a good fit. You can sign with more than one agency if you want to work in differing mediums. It all goes back to the idea that you don't have to be everything for everyone. For example, it is not uncommon for a versatile performer to be represented as a singer/dancer by one agency and a commercial actress by another, etc. As long as both agencies aren't sending you out on the same types of auditions, there isn't a conflict of interest.

## HOW TO KEEP AN AGENT

Once you get an agent, you must make a concerted effort to maintain your relationship with him or her. Check in fairly often to stay in their consciousness. Share information. Show up to your audition appointments. Stay on top of your game and keep up your skills. Set actual career goals so they know where to focus. Appreciate the work they put in and make an effort to follow through on your end. Keep them updated with your availability. For example, if you are planning a trip out of town, give them ample notice so they can avoid submitting you for something you are not available for (that's referred to as "booking out."). Be honest. Work together.

Lucille DiCampli is a partner and the director of the New York office of MacDonald/Selznick Associates, an agency specializing in dancers and choreographers with offices in L.A. and N.Y. She shared this insight into the agent/client relationship:

*Anyone is ready for an agent if they are ready to make adjustments to their life. It's about prioritizing. When you are still non-union and overcommit yourself and can't make the auditions I get for you, that's not a good thing when you first sign on. You have to make yourself available. I'm your business partner. If you don't get that and I am the last person to know anything, it bothers me. It's about communicating. We are going to get there, but we've got to be in it together and all of the effort can't be on the part of my office. When all you say is "I want to be a star!" but can't tell me how you want to get there, I am not the right agent for you. If you say, "I want to be on Broadway!" but aren't studying to improve your voice or better your dance skills, I'm not an agent for you because you aren't serious about it. This is a refined art. If you aren't focused and sure of what you want to do, I am not a good fit.*

# MANAGERS

Managers are similar to agents in that they are in the business of helping artists develop their careers over time, but more specialized in that they manage more than auditions and contracts. Managers may specialize in representing a certain type of performer, and the good ones tend to have a small, limited number of clients whom they focus on solely. He or she will submit you for various projects and auditions, sometimes working in conjunction with an agent to do so, but will also take additional interest in helping you focus on a specific type of work and develop your career over the long term. Managers can pitch you to casting directors, get you into the classes or with coaches who will help to better prepare you, life coach, take charge of your schedule, develop your look and marketing strategies, review scripts and potential projects, generate and use publicity, secure endorsements, and help you to meet and network with people who will take your career further.

At higher levels, managers may work with a publicist (whom you will also pay) to promote you across the media. For all of this, managers generally make a commission of 15 to 20% of all your related earnings. If you and your manager are also working with an agent, that agent will also get 10%, which means up to 30% of your earnings (before taxes, which can be another 25% in some states) will be paid out to the people working with you. For those earning higher fees, all of these payouts can be worth it.

One major difference between agents and managers is that managers are not licensed by the state or franchised by unions. This means they are not subject to the same regulations that an agent is. This can be an advantage in that they can be more involved in your life and career on a personal level, but also adverse in that they can make up their own rules without oversight. Make sure your contract with a manager is very specific and clear as to responsibilities, payouts, and duration. There are excellent, very legitimate, and professional managers in the industry who have helped countless performers succeed. There are also some hacks you should steer clear of; always do your research into a manager's work history and reputation prior to signing. Don't just take a manager's word for it. You must be a wise investor.

## HOW TO GET A MANAGER

The process of seeking a manager is similar to the way one would find an agent. Networking is, again, the best way to get a meeting, but managers also attend showcases and performances seeking new talent. Some respond to postcard and headshot mailings.

Managers specialize in a variety of artists. Recording artists, directors, choreographers, designers, actors who are principals in film/TV and major theater, celebrities, models, opera singers, headliners, and specialty acts (or new professionals wanting to pursue those fields) all may see careers develop further with the help of a manager. Performers hoping to move out of ensemble work and into leading or principal roles might find the services of a manager helpful in making that transition. Most performers who work primarily in ensemble-type jobs don't use managers, though there is no rule saying they can't. Knowing what your career goals are is an important element for determining what kind of manager is best for you.

## STRIP MALL SCAMS

You have no doubt seen the talent agency mall kiosks luring in potential clients with the promise of fame and success. If you sign on as "a client," the manager will represent you, but only after you have purchased a headshot/modeling portfolio package and several class series or coaching sessions through the agency. Once you invest several thousand dollars in the agency, these *non-licensed* talent managers will begin submitting you for film, TV, and print jobs. These companies are selling a product—and that product is not you. It is possible that the classes are decent or the headshots will be great, but launching a career as a performer is not as easy as shopping at the mall. Beware of an agency that asks for fees in advance. Commissions to legitimate managers or agents are paid only after work has been booked, completed, and paid for by a producer. Contact the Better Business Bureau to learn more about these strip mall agency chains, or better yet, invest your money in a legitimate school of training in the first place.

## THINGS TO KNOW WHEN SEEKING REPRESENTATION

Knowing when and why to attain the services of a manager or agent is dependent upon your own market analysis and career goals. Having a manager or agent is not a necessity to achieve a career in certain mediums, but in others, it may open doors that would otherwise be unavailable to you. In the search for ideal representation, there are several factors to take into consideration.

- If the person is legitimate, you will *not* be asked for any money up front. Agents and managers only make commissions off the work you book while you're under an agreement or contract with them.

- The agent should be licensed and franchised. Managers are not required to have a license, so you must be more cautious.

- It is still your career. You are the decision maker. You don't work for your agent/manager. You work with them in the mutual interests of your own career. The final decisions are yours, but you must take everyone's investment into account.

- Good communication is *everything*. It is your job to stay in touch with your agent and manager more so than it is theirs. Check in with them often, let them know if you receive information before they do, and always keep the office updated if you are going to be out of town or unavailable.

- Freelancing[38] with an agent or manager for a period of time is not uncommon. It might be right for you. It might also be like dating without commitment, and you could be quickly forgotten. Freelance clients cannot expect to receive the same amount of attention a signed client does. Be realistic about what freelancing means, and talk to other performers about their freelancing experiences with specific agents or managers.

- If you sign with an agent or manager, the hard work is not over for you. An agent works for 10%. That means 90% of the effort is still your responsibility. You will need to hustle, network, go to class, and work just as hard at finding success as you did before. The difference is that you have someone on your side to help lend some support.

---

[38] Freelancing: Working with an agent or manager without actually signing an exclusive contract. Some use it as a way to "try someone out" and see how it goes.

- Don't expect an agent or manager to work for free. If you are not putting in the work or booking the jobs, don't be surprised if your agent or manager drops you from representation. People work to earn a living, not as a hobby. You shouldn't expect your agent to starve just because you are! They may need to concentrate their efforts on the clients who pay their bills. Remember, it's "show *business*."

Jeremy Leiner is a talent agent with Nicolosi and Co., Inc., a boutique agency based in New York City. He represents legit actors for film, television, and theater. I asked Jeremy what advice he had to pass on to young professionals interested in seeking representation.

### How should the size of an agency affect a performer's decision about whom to sign with?

JL:     *Deciding who represents you is a very personal decision. The size of an agency often refers to the number of agents who work at the office and the number of clients they represent. It does not refer to their reach within the industry. Who is excited to pick up the phone to talk about you and whom do you trust? Who do you feel comfortable discussing the choices in your career with and who believes in you for the long haul rather than just the bottom line? No matter the size of the agency, who will make the best pitch to get you into those [audition] rooms?*

### What does someone need to do when submitting materials to a new agent?

JL:     *I look at every piece mail I receive, so if you are going to send your materials, snail mail is best. Unless you are a referral from a client or casting director, please do not e-mail me, because it will get lost in the enormous amounts of e-mail I receive every day, or worse, deleted. That said, a headshot and resume is simply not enough information to generate interest in representing someone. I must somehow see your work, be it a reel, YouTube/Vimeo links, or even better you performing in something you are proud of that features you. If you just booked a role on a TV show and added the scenes to your reel, or are going on for a principal role in a Broadway or off-Broadway show, I want to know about it. I do not need to know how many callbacks you have had, or that you*

*d for a commercial. I respond most to clear, specific, and professional*
*s, rather than silly, cutesy, or kitschy ones. Also, when sending*
*any agent, please do your research. For example, I represent adult*
*signed only basis for legit TV / theater/ film work. If you are*
*looking for commercial representation, or your 12-year-old daughter is the next*
*Meryl Streep, I am simply not the agent for you.*

**What are some tips for having a successful working relationship with an agent?**

JL:    *When an actor signs with me out of school, I encourage them to be just as much*
*a part of the "team" as I am. Most graduates are used to a student/professor*
*relationship, rooted in hierarchy and respect. While respect will remain, I want*
*my clients to even out the relationship and level the playing field. Think of it*
*this way: when you graduate, you become a business owner:* Your Name
Here, Inc. *Every great company needs a president and CEO (you) and a*
*board of trustees (your agents). It is my job to bring you wonderful*
*opportunities, but together we will make decisions about your business and*
*career. It is your job to be an active and communicative member of your*
*team. Do not withhold information from your agents. They may already be in*
*the know, but remember that they are in an office every day while you are out in*
*the trenches. It is important to let your agents know about projects you hear*
*about and are interested in, people you meet and have worked with, and any*
*talking points that might be helpful (i.e., your brother-in-law is the producer). I*
*want to be as informed as possible when pitching you for a project.*

# UNIONS

The labor union movement that grew out of the industrial age in the
United States did so to ensure that workers received fair wages, worked
regular hours, and could be guaranteed standard working conditions. Before
unions for performing artists began, it was not uncommon for performers
to be told to work in unsafe environments, asked to work many hours at a
time with no break, and stranded out of town with no salary if a show
closed unexpectedly. When professional New York actors banded together

over 100 years ago to create Actors' Equity Association, they forced producers to treat their artists with professional respect and dignity and create safe and fair working conditions.

## REASONS TO JOIN A UNION

The labor unions for performing artists essentially do what the labor unions in other industries do. They negotiate collective bargaining agreements[39] with producers that include salary minimums, hours of rehearsal and breaks, stage/studio conditions, safety issues, cleanliness standards, housing and travel, compensation for additional duties, benefit contributions, job retention, and much more. The union requires a producer to put up a prepaid bond so that, should a show close early, performers are not stranded away from home without pay or transportation. It also requires that performers be given ample closing notice.

Unions have a variety of collective bargaining agreements with various producers or collectives of producers. Salaries and provisions vary according to medium, size of the production, etc., and each union provides a current list of contracts available on their websites.

Unions ensure there will be open auditions for union performers, franchise talent agents, and provide members access to health insurance, a pension, a 401(k), disability insurance, workers' compensation, and emergency funds among other benefits. Your name is protected; only one person in a union at a time can professionally use a specific name.

## THE FOUR UNIONS FOR PERFORMING ARTISTS

There are four separate unions covering performers in various mediums, and you may belong to more than one. All four are affiliated with and support their sister unions as members of the AFL-CIO. They also stand with the unions covering other industry professionals, honoring each other's picket lines. They share a credit union and support industry charities including The Actors Fund and BC/EFA.

---

[39] Collective bargaining agreement: A standard contract that applies to all union members working on a specific job. The union negotiates the contract with the producer on behalf of all members, and both sides must adhere to the terms.

- **Actors' Equity Association (AEA)**

This is the union for professional stage actors and stage managers and the oldest of the four. This union covers actors, singers, and dancers performing on stage in book musicals and plays. All Broadway shows, some national tours, many regional theaters, and more operate under Equity agreements. To join the union, you must either work 50 weeks with regional/stock theaters who offer "Equity Membership Candidate" points (each workweek equals one point) or be given an Equity contract outright when hired for a show. You pay an initiation fee and annual dues. Weekly 2% working dues and benefit payments are taken out of your paychecks. Health insurance is available after a minimum number of work weeks on an Equity contract per year. Members also have a pension and 401(k) opportunities. Members may not work in book shows[40] on stage that are non-union within the United States. All union jobs must hold open auditions available to any union member. These are called EPAs (Equity Principal Auditions for leading and principal roles) and ECCs (Equity Chorus Calls for ensemble roles). Visit www.actorsequity.org for more information.

- **Screen Actors Guild and American Federation of Television and Radio Artists (SAG-AFTRA)**

This is the union for professional performers in film, television, radio, and web series. It also covers some models, newscasters and sportscasters. This union resulted recently when two unions (SAG and AFTRA) merged into one. Most feature films, television series, and major market commercials operate under SAG-AFTRA contracts. To join the union, you must either have proof of employment (a voucher or pay stub) that proves you worked in a position covered by a SAG-AFTRA collective bargaining agreement (three days if a background extra) or been a member of a sister union for one year (AEA, AGMA, AGVA, ACTRA in Canada) and performed and been paid on a principal contract. You pay an initiation fee and annual dues, and have working dues, healthcare contributions, and pension taken out of your paychecks. Members may not perform in film and television without a union contract worldwide. Visit www.sagaftra.org for more information.

---

[40] Book shows: These are shows with a clear, scripted storyline as opposed to a revue format which may be a collection of songs with a theme or a series of vignettes.

- **American Guild of Variety Artists (AGVA)**
This union represents performing artists and stage managers for live performances in the variety field including theatrical revues, theme parks, circus, comedians, lecturers, and skaters. *The Radio City Christmas Spectacular*, Disneyland, some non-book shows on Broadway, and Universal Studios Hollywood theme park all operate under AGVA agreements. You may join the union if you are offered an AGVA contract or a member in good standing with a sister union. Individual variety acts may also apply to be reviewed for membership. You pay working dues three times per year. Health insurance plans are available. AGVA members may work non-AGVA jobs. Visit www.agvausa.com for more information.

- **American Guild of Musical Artists (AGMA)**
This is the union for performers and other creative artists in opera companies, chorales, and dance companies. Large companies such as the Metropolitan Opera, American Ballet Theatre, Alvin Ailey American Dance Theatre, San Francisco Ballet, L.A. Opera, and more operate under AGMA agreements. AGMA is an open enrollment union, meaning to join you must only apply. You pay an initiation fee, as well as annual/basic and working dues. Health insurance/savings accounts are available. AGMA members are free to work both union and non-union jobs. Visit www.musicalartists.org for more information.

## REASONS *NOT* TO JOIN A UNION

There are no restricted opportunities to work as a performer if you are not under a union's jurisdiction. Many union theaters hire non-union performers for reduced rates. You avoid paying dues and may receive health and pension benefits from certain employers instead. There are still opportunities to audition at Equity-only auditions, though you might wait a long time to be seen. If you are not living and working in New York or Los Angeles, or if you live in a right-to-work state in general, being a union member might limit the number of jobs available to you in your local area too much. You have to evaluate your market and your own goals as a performer. Choosing not to join a union does not diminish the contributions that unions make on behalf of performers nor does it make you an illegitimate professional. Even if your goal is to eventually join a union, don't join before your career is ready. You could be limiting your ability to grow.

## WHEN *TO* JOIN THE UNION

This is the question that troubles many young professionals. Attaining a union membership card ("getting your card"[41]) is a big accomplishment for a professional. It takes work and perseverance. Most of the bigger jobs are covered with union agreements. The right time to join is different for everyone, and you should carefully analyze your career in order to know when that time is for you. Ask seasoned professionals their opinions about your career specifically and seek more than one opinion. Know your market and the ratio of union contract availability, remembering that working non-union when you first start out definitely opens up more work opportunities.

Gaining professional experience is an important part of your training—amassing non-union weeks at Equity regional theaters, performing in a non-union national tour, or gaining experience on a union film set will help you develop your skills and build your needed network. Taking your card "too soon" could mean denying yourself these work opportunities while also being limited to stiff competition with seasoned professionals before you've had time to sharpen your audition skills. A decrease in chances to work could limit the development of your professional skills.

On the other hand, you may already be booking all union jobs at a young age, which is a good sign that you are ready to join. Some unions require that you join after working a certain number of union jobs anyway.

Here's my best advice: allow your card to find you. When the time is right, it will do just that. Set yourself up by working to earn your weeks or vouchers and auditioning for union jobs, but when you are new to the business, embrace the freedom to take non-union work if it interests you. Build the network that is going to aide you once you do join a union. As

---

[41] Getting your card: Joining a performer's union by receiving a contract and paying your initiation fees which results in your membership card being sent to you in the mail.

you continue in the business, the time to take your card will become obvious. Remember, it is not a race! The time is different for everyone, and you don't have to rush to get your card just because your friend did.

## THE BENEFITS OF JOINING A UNION

If it makes sense for the market you are in, eventually joining one or more of the unions is a great goal. You will earn more money doing the jobs you do. As independent contractors, joining is a way to have consistent health insurance, a pension, a 401(k), and other benefits that continue across your time with multiple employers. There are professional services available for free (i.e., income tax accounting services) and discounts at various retailers. Joining is a way to attain better wages, overtime fees, scheduled breaks, days off, cleanliness standards, and safety provisions without having to negotiate for each line in a contract individually. Union membership offers great networking opportunities and access to members-only auditions where you are guaranteed to be seen without waiting all day. Joining means you are working alongside other artists who excel in your field and that you are one of them.

No union is perfect, but each is governed solely by its members. You can be as involved as you want to be in how your union is run. From the performers perspective, we are better off with unions than without. They were created for a reason!

# ACCOUNTANTS

You are a small business and your tax returns can become complicated, involving multiple forms. At the end of the year, you may have worked many jobs and received several W-2 and 1099 forms from different employers in different states. Some performers choose to form their own corporations for tax purposes, but that tends to happen later in a career, if ever. As freelancers, a majority of performers are considered sole proprietors. There are many who are completely capable of maintaining their own bookkeeping. In fact, you should make it a point to keep track of your own receipts and expenses as a small business owner. When it comes to actually filing your taxes, you might be someone who understands the tax code or an online tax program—good for you!—but not everyone is comfortable calculating his or her own taxes and will choose to hire a professional. That is normal too. There are accountants, especially in the major markets, who specialize in filing taxes specifically for performers. Union members have access to free tax services with tax professionals in the major cities through programs like VITA.[42] It is important that you use an accountant who understands the expenses associated with the entertainment business and what write-offs apply to your specific profession. Rely on your network for referrals.

## THE PERFORMING ARTIST TAX CODE

There is an IRS code for those who identify as "performing artists" and, in addition to all of the standard deductions you are eligible for as a U.S. citizen/legal alien, there are several business-related expenses that you can write off against your income as a result of pursuing and performing work as an artist. Expenses are applicable both in your home state as well as when you are working "on the road." It is important to save receipts, bank statements, credit card bills, paid checks, tip/expense journals, check stubs, and other forms of payment verification throughout the year. This record keeping is critical. If you are ever audited, you must have the proof of all expenditures available and organized. You also don't want to lose out on any expenses for which you qualify. Specifics may vary from year to year, but the unions always maintain an up-to-date list of acceptable expenses. As of the time this book was written, the list of acceptable expenses for performing artists include:

- **Advertising/Publicity**: Headshot photo sessions and reproductions, business cards, stationery, postcards, online professional registries, demo reels, business website fees.

---

[42] VITA: an IRS-sponsored tax assistance program that was initiated by Equity in the 1970s. It is run on a volunteer basis by IRS-trained members and provides free tax preparation to paid-up members of Equity and other performing arts unions. There are currently programs at the Equity office in New York and the AFTRA office in Seattle.

- **Apparel**: Costumes, dance shoes, theatrical makeup and wigs as well as the cleaning, altering and repair of work-related apparel. "Audition clothes" may or may not qualify depending upon what they are.

- **Auto/transportation expenses:** Can apply in-town or "on the road." Round-trip mileage to auditions as well as airfare, bus fare, car rental, lodging, tips, parking, taxi, and subway fares related to the pursuit of work.

- **Equipment**: Includes computers, printers, ear prompters, etc. Equipment purchased is generally "depreciated" and written off over five to seven years.

- **Gifts for business**: Gifts given to colleagues with whom you have professional relationships. Only $25.00 value per year per person is deductible.

- **Home office**: If you use a room in your home *exclusively* for your business, you could qualify for a home office deduction. The room can be a rehearsal space, teaching space, home recording and/or video studio, record keeping for the business, marketing, etc. You can write off a percentage of associated costs like rent, mortgage interest, real estate taxes, condo fees, utilities, insurance, repairs, etc.

- **Legal and professional fees**: Commissions to agents and managers, attorney fees, tax preparation, and union dues.

- **Meals:** Business-related meals are 50% deductible. They must include direct business discussions or occur when on the road for work.

- **Tickets for professional research**: Admissions for theatrical productions or film screenings that you can justify attending for professional reasons.

- **Training**: Acting, voice, dance lessons, or other education related to improving or maintaining your performance skills. This also includes rental fees for rehearsal space. People try, but you cannot write off gym memberships...

- **Supplies**: Ink cartages, headshot reproductions, mailing supplies, makeup, fax and photocopy fees, postage and subscriptions to industry publications.

Please consult the current listings of qualifying expenses published by the IRS for verification. Save all of your receipts in each category and keep good records—make it a habit! Your accountant can help you determine what you can use and what you can't, but if you don't have receipts they will have nothing to go off of.

# ENTERTAINMENT LAWYERS

Most young performers will never require the services of an entertainment lawyer. Attorneys who specialize in entertainment law are more of a necessity for performers working at very high-income levels, who are dealing with creative copyrights and international contracts, or who are unique and creating a deal that has never been done or tried before. Paying a lawyer to review your theme park or cruise line contract is a waste of your money as the terms will always be fairly standard.

If you should become involved in career-related litigation for any reason, you may need their services. The unions also retain the services of entertainment lawyers on behalf of their members in certain situations.

# Chapter Seven

# Career Longevity

*"Remember that it's work—it's not play. We're lucky we love what we do, but it is still work and this job is always about the next job. Once you're in a gig, your job is to do so well that they love working with you and can't wait to have you back. There are a million things to consider other than just dancing and singing."*

**-Peggy Hickey, choreographer for theater, film, television and opera**

Peggy gave me this exact advice early in my career, and it has always stuck with me. When you are a professional, it is not about booking just one job—it's about sustaining a career. Your talent is your product, but the person you put out there can make all the difference in how often your talent is allowed to shine. You have choices. You can choose to conduct yourself in a professional manner on the job. You can choose the way you interact with others. You can choose to be a person whom others will want to work with again and again.

When determining whether or not to rehire a performer, Jodie Stinebaugh, casting director for Stiletto Entertainment, considers several factors:

*Unfortunately, there are those performers that I do not bring back for additional contracts. Obviously, a serious offense such as drug and/or alcohol abuse is grounds for a "no-rehire status"; however, many other things come into play. Was the performer respectful to choreographers, musical directors, crew, and fellow castmates? Did he/she take direction? Was his/her performance consistent? Did he/she maintain costumes and wigs? Did he/she maintain his/her look (i.e., hair color and weight)? Was he/she on time for calls? There is more to this gig than being a fantastic and talented performer.*

For professionals who are just starting out, surviving throughout the length of a contract takes some navigating. Sometimes a cast will just click from day one, the show will feel great, and it's smooth sailing right to the end. You will love these jobs and will be sad when they end. Other times there will be too many conflicting personalities off stage, complicated politics, or administrative issues that make the workplace feel miserable. It happens to everyone. In that case, take the experience for what it is, learn what you can, perform your best, maintain your professionalism, and do what you can to avoid being a part of the problem.

Your reputation is what will precede you, and you ultimately have control over your own behavior. Patti Colombo, an Emmy-nominated L.A.-based choreographer and director, strongly considers reputations when she is hiring.

> *You aren't a star just because you've shown up. It's important to stay humble and have grace as a performer. We all know how small the business is. I take it very seriously when someone I trust warns me about the bad behavior of a performer. It makes me not want to work with them.*

People make mistakes. Over and over, those who have come before you have learned lessons the hard way. You don't have to do the same. The following tips, collected from the experiences of a variety of seasoned entertainment professionals, are all things to take to heart. Other professionals may assume you already know these things when working in a professional environment even though they are not necessarily inherent to your studies.

# THE 25 "UNWRITTEN" RULES OF PROFESSIONALISM

1. **Every performance is important.** The reality of performing in a long run of a show can be a bit jarring for young performers. Where before you may have been used to a run of two weeks at most, you will now find yourself in a run of six months or longer. Some performers fall into a habit of giving a lesser performance on some days ("phoning it in") and a full-out performance on others. There is a difference between pacing yourself across a week and consciously giving an altered performance from one show to the next. As a professional, it is your job to give consistent performances that are full and maintain the artistic intent and integrity you were hired to deliver every time. Additionally, the final show of the run is not a "free-for-all." It is not time for onstage hijinks and antics. That paying audience deserves to see the same show.

2. **Everyone has a job to do.** Respect that everyone is there to perform a vital function and that everyone's contribution is equally important to the overall product. Treat your fellow cast members with respect. Treat management with respect. Above all, treat all crew members (stage crew, dressers, board and spot operators, grips, cameramen, etc.) with respect. They are not there to serve you. They are there to work too. The audience might be watching you onstage, but a show without each valued crew member would just be you performing naked in the dark.

3. **Mind your own business, not the business of others.** Never give a fellow performer a note on something you feel they are doing wrong. If they are doing something different that affects your performance, talk to your dance captain, stage manager, or assistant director/choreographer. If you are having a partnering issue, go to your dance captain first. Never give line readings or blocking notes. If a fellow cast member is doing a dance move on a wrong count or paraphrasing a line, etc., but it is *not* directly

affecting your performance, keep it to yourself and allow management to find it and handle it. That's their job. On the flip side, if you are receiving notes from another actor, do bring it to management's attention. Your management team is responsible for maintaining the entire show; you are responsible for maintaining your own performance.

4. **Ask but don't demand**. If you need something in order to deliver the best performance possible (a fixed prop, repaired shoes, a non-slippery deck, an ice pack, etc.), it's okay to ask. When you deal with management, remember there is a difference between asking for what you need and causing drama by making demands. Use your manners and remain a calm professional even if you don't get the answer you want.

5. **Take the note**. You will inevitably get notes from management about your performances throughout the run. Everyone gets notes. It is an important part of the show maintenance process. There is an art to accepting and applying a note gracefully. When you are given a note, the professional response is either "thank you" or "I'm not sure what you mean—can you please explain?" (Then "thank you" after the note has been more clearly explained.) Then, apply that note in the next performance. Contrary to what some believe, notes are not personal judgments. Dance captains and stage managers are not your enemies. Good artists tend to be perfectionists but must learn to accept constructive criticism. If you are doing a step on the wrong count, it is not the end of the world. It's only a step—if asked, just fix it. Maybe you have morphed it; maybe you remember it being taught differently; maybe the dance captain is refining a movement so everyone matches. It doesn't matter if you think you have been doing it right and "their change" is wrong—just take the note. They have been empowered by the creative team to clean things. You don't have to announce to the cast that you feel it is a change—an unwavering need to make yourself sound "right" might impress your own ego but never a room full of colleagues. And it does not serve the artistic quality of the piece!

6. **Keep organized and communicate clearly.** Stay up to date with show times, half-hour calls[43], put-in and cleaning rehearsals, publicity calls, and any other job-related events that affect your schedule. Stage managers, ADs and company managers will keep you informed throughout the run or shoot of specifics and changes. Do your best to keep your dressing room station neat and your belongings confined to your allotted area. Answer phone messages and emails in a timely fashion when business is involved. It could mean the difference between booking a job or being considered in the future.

7. **Stay healthy.** Your body is your instrument and your livelihood. Everyone is depending on you to take care of it. Stay in shape. Maintain the size and shape you were hired with. Continue to warm up before shows, stretch regularly, eat right, take class, go to the gym, and cross train. Doing the same show every night for a long period of time can cause wear and tear on your muscles. Most young professionals don't realize the stamina it takes to maintain a consistent performance over the long term. Performing eight or more shows a week for 50 weeks out of the year can be grueling. Pace yourself. Don't waste energy unnecessarily. Be conscious of your diet. Drink lots of water. And, it should go without saying, never show up to work under the influence of alcohol or drugs. That is dangerous for everyone.

8. **Call out[44] when necessary.** Know when to "call out" of a show if you need to. Swings and understudies exist for a reason. If you are sick or injured and unable to fulfill your performance duties in a

---

[43] Half-hour call: In Equity stage productions, performers are required by contract to be at the theater no later than 30 minutes prior to the curtain time. Some shows may require a call time earlier than a half hour.

[44] Call out: the shortened version of "calling out sick." If a performer is too ill to perform, there may be provisions in place where the performer can stay home from work and take a sick day either paid or unpaid (just like in any other legitimate profession).

healthy way on a given evening, it is okay to call out. Your fellow performers will appreciate that you are preventing them from getting ill or jeopardizing a lift or movement because of an unfortunate injury. On the flip side, refrain from abusing the fact that there are understudies and swings. Call out when you need to, not just when you want to. If you are working on a project without understudies or swings, immediately notify your stage manager and dance captain if you are ill so they can make necessary modifications.

9. **Be on time for your calls.** This applies not only to getting to work by or before your official call time, but getting to your sound check or wig/makeup calls as well. There are tight schedules created for you to follow that affect the work of others. People rely on your promptness to keep things efficient. Avoid costing the project time. And if circumstances beyond your control cause you to be late, notify your stage manager immediately so that schedules can be adjusted accordingly.

10. **Respect the work.** Have respect for what is being done onstage, whether you are also onstage or in the wings. Yes, theater should be fun and you must keep it fresh with each performance, but things like breaking character, talking loudly upstage, giggling, whispering, having loud discussions in the wings, or altering the choreography, blocking, or business for your own amusement, etc., robs the audience of the performance they paid to see. Each time you cause a lapse in focus onstage, you burden someone else in the cast with the task of getting the audience back. Respect your fellow actors and the people paying to be transported.

11. **Respect your audience.** Every audience member is choosing to spend his/her time and money attending your performance. They all deserve a full show performed with artistic integrity and intent whether the house is sold out or not. Remember that at every performance, there is one person in the audience experiencing live theater for the first time and one person experiencing it for the last.

12. **Respect your elders**. When you have the privilege of working with veteran professionals, embrace the opportunity. They may no longer have the advantage of learning lines quickly or remembering blocking on the spot, but they were once you. They embody a lifetime of knowledge. You can learn a lot from them about the business and artistry. Young saplings are exciting to nurture and see grow, but the big, beautiful trees are the strongest and most valuable.

13. **Understand your purpose in the story telling**. For leads and principals, this is usually easy. If you are in the ensemble on stage, working as background on set, dancing behind a musical artist, or playing a supporting role onscreen, you need to approach the work knowing the function of your role and respect others in regards to that purpose. You might be moving the plot forward by how you react; you might be creating the realistic atmosphere where the story lives; you might be framing the lead; you might have an action the lead is relying on. Your role wouldn't exist if it wasn't important—you're there for a reason even if the moment is not specifically about you.

14. **Understand your medium**. The simplest things in the world can quickly turn a professional show into an amateur one. On stage, be aware of sightlines and the fact that curtains and scrims are not soundproof. When exiting with people behind you, don't stop short in the wings so that others cannot get cleanly offstage. Keep walking until you get to the dressing room! Don't touch the rail line sets. Don't whistle or say the "M" word[45] in a theater even if you are not superstitious.

15. **Hang up your own costumes**. Obviously this may not apply to quick changes, but when changing in your dressing room or trailer,

---

[45] "M" word: In theater it is bad luck to utter the word "Macbeth." It is referred to instead as "The Scottish Play." The superstition dates back to the original Shakespearean production. An actor is said to have been killed when a real dagger was used instead of a prop dagger. Productions of *Macbeth* are notorious for having "accidents," and it is believed that saying the title will bring that same bad luck down upon whatever production you are working on.

take a minute to hang up your own costumes after you have taken them off. A minute of thoughtfulness from each performer can save an hour of work for the wardrobe crew. Be courteous.

16. **Don't be a diva.** Artists are passionate people. In a professional situation you will be asked to work with a variety of strong personalities, and you may not always agree with everyone. Remember that patience is a virtue. Egos should be kept in check. Tempers can be controlled. Deal with conflict using as much professional courtesy as you can muster. "Blowing up" at someone in the moment out of pride may prevent you from being respected in the present or hired in the future. People remember…. Ask yourself if the future backlash is worth that one egotistical moment.

17. **Leave your personal problems outside.** Come to work prepared to work. Artists are emotionally driven people, and sometimes it is hard to leave personal issues (i.e., relationship issues, etc.) at the door. Learn to do so. Talk it out with your friends on the lunch break or in the bar after work, but do not burden the working environment unnecessarily. If you are coming to work, find your focus.

18. **Never cost the project time and money.** Film and television productions are costly, and a week of shooting can run in the millions. Every time an actor shows up unprepared, flubs a line, misses a mark, cracks up in a scene, or prematurely causes the director to yell "Cut!" because of an avoidable mistake, that actor is wasting time and money. Every unusable take costs money. Every retake costs money. Every time people on set are sitting around waiting for you to get it together, it costs money.

19. **Mind your "Ps and Qs."** Dressing rooms are cesspools for gossip. If you must gossip, only do so in the privacy of your own life away from work and your colleagues. Or just fight the urges altogether. When you gossip about others behind their backs, it will inevitably get back to them. In a social business like ours, that can be detrimental. The tension you cause in a cast affects the entire

company. People remember... Don't cause drama. Don't buy into other people's drama. Just be a good company member.

20. **Behave "on the road."** If you are doing a job away from home, you will likely be living, eating, breathing your cast outside of work. Make wise choices when you socialize. Certainly be yourself; however, consider yourself somewhat still "at work" when you are out with your colleagues. Have a lot of fun—being on the road is a blast!—but don't find yourself completely out of control. (Yes, I am speaking to the partiers. You know who you are!) Your reputation is everything, so choose the image you put out there.

21. **Keep it positive.** Nothing can poison the workplace faster than backstage negativity. Dissing your own show, bringing up negative reviews, and negatively commenting on another's performance shows a lack of respect for a work in process. Don't be the person who brings down the experience for everyone else. The chronic complainers, backstabbers, mean girls, and Debbie downers can make the dressing room a downright toxic place.

22. **There is no entitlement.** This is a biggie. When a generation is raised to believe "everyone gets a trophy no matter what," it is no wonder a person has a sense that he or she is owed success simply by being. I wish the real world of show business worked the way your childhood did—but it doesn't. If the feelings that you "deserve" every job you audition for or that you are just "more talented" than everyone else are frequent for you, learn to manage those feelings. They will *never* serve you. Use some humility to change your outlook. Direct your energy toward a healthy, positive, collaborative work ethic instead; otherwise, the inevitable rejections of the business will torture you and everyone who has to deal with you.

23. **Know when to leave.** Most contracts you sign will be for a finite amount of time. If you are cast in an open-ended show, however, it is important for you to know when it is time to leave. There are those performers who can perform in the same show eight times a

week for 10 years straight. I applaud them! That was never "me." Artists tend to need new ways to express themselves. It's how we grow. If you are feeling the urge to spread your wings and it is beginning to affect your feelings in a negative way toward your show, cast, or workplace, then it's time for you to give notice and move on. Hopefully, you will book a new job to move into, but if not, you may need to give your notice anyway. Know yourself as an artist. Make sure you follow the protocol in your contract and leave on good terms.

24. **Don't burn your bridges.** You may not like every director you work with. You might not like how a producer runs his company while you work there. You may think a choreographer's work is terrible. You are entitled to your opinion. It will not serve you well to share that opinion with those people—don't let them walk away with a bad taste for you even if you have a bad taste for them. Leave them with the impression that you are a hard worker who delivers an excellent and consistent performance. You can choose not to audition or work for them again while at the same time leave the door open for them to recommend you to someone else. It's a small world…

25. **Attitude is everything!** It's always about the next job. The more everyone in the room enjoys working with you, the more likely you are to work with each of them again multiple times. Your reputation is important, and you control it through the choices you make. You never know where your next job might come from, and many jobs can come from word-of-mouth recommendations. Be someone that other people can't wait to work with again!

Embrace these rules and set a path for career longevity. You may find yourself working with other artists, theaters, and production companies again and again.

# THE LEAD SETS THE TONE

If you are lucky enough to be cast in a leading role, there is great responsibility that comes with that position both on and off stage. Whether working in theater, film, or television, a leading performer needs to understand the position he or she is in. You will have great responsibility for carrying a show on your shoulders on stage or on set, but you also have the responsibility of leading a company off stage in rehearsal and backstage. Company morale comes down from the top, and you have the ability to control it or sabotage it. Being a "diva" is rarely a sign of status, and more often than not it's a sign of great insecurity. If you set a good example of behavior, work ethic, and grace, others will follow you.

Judith Blazer has been a leading lady for much of her distinguished career. On and off-Broadway, she has played leading roles in *Me & My Girl, A Change In the Heir, Titanic,* Neil Simon's *45 Seconds from Broadway, LoveMusik* directed by Harold Prince, *Hello Again, The Torch Bearers,* and *The House of Bernarda Alba*; lead roles for New York City Opera in *Candide* and *Sweeney Todd*; principal characters on soap operas *As the World Turns* and *The Guiding Light*; guest soloist performances for regional symphonies and The Metropolitan Opera; and title roles in regional theater including "Eliza Dolittle" in *My Fair Lady,* "Fanny Brice" in *Funny Girl,* and "Annie Sullivan" in *The Miracle Worker.* She has truly done it all and has a glowing industry reputation! Judy continues to perform while teaching young theater and voice students through her private studio in New York and her educational program, The Artists' Crossing.

*A leading lady, or leading man, sets the tone of the work from the very first day. If you're smart you are setting moods for what you are going to do later. There are the obvious things—have the proper rehearsal clothes, understand that your body is your instrument, be there before the downbeat, be ready to go. But, as a lead, you must also be warm and welcoming to every cast member. You treat everyone in the cast with importance. You not only know everyone's names but you look into all of their eyes when you are with them on stage. You acknowledge them the way the host at a party would. A leading player has to understand they are no better or more important as a human being nor artist creating the work than anyone else. They have to understand the ensemble is standing behind them not receiving the glory, perhaps not receiving the same pay, but having to work sometimes twice as hard.*

*I remember saying to my last Henry Higgins, "Look at all these talented people dancing and singing and playing all of these characters and changing their clothes 50 million times. I'm not good enough to be in the ensemble. That's why I'm a leading lady." I have been in the ensemble only a few times in my career, and I have seen the wrath of what it is when the leading lady doesn't treat you with the same grace.*

# IT'S ALL ABOUT RELATIONSHIPS

People like to work with people they know and enjoy—your professional relationships can help to make (or break) your career. If you enjoyed your experience on a certain job and you know that others enjoyed working with you too, keep in touch with those directors, choreographers, artistic directors, producers, and casting directors with whom you felt a connection. Consider it a part of your job to tell them about what you are doing, and express interest in working with them in the future. By keeping up with the projects they are working on, you will be able to ask if you can audition for specific roles you are right for. You may find yourself working with the same people several times throughout your professional life.

**Be in the moment, both onstage and off.** Connecting with the other artists you work with requires that you engage and be open not only within a scene but within a work environment. Jason Graae, who created the role of "Sparky" in *Forever Plaid* and voiced "Lucky the Leprechaun" for Lucky Charms cereal commercials among many other credits, stresses the importance for performers to connect with each other while in the creative process.

*The phones. The Phones. The PHONES! Acting and the theatre are so much about being in the moment. It's the art of discovery. It's about developing relationships on and off stage. So many people are so hyper-concerned with texting, Tweeting, and Facebooking (on every break!) that it takes them out of the present moment. Don't get me wrong—I love the technology. I'm a Facebook whore. And I use all of it to market. But there's a time and place.*

**You don't need to be everything to everyone.** As you continue to grow professionally, you will find that you can strategize your career in certain areas based on your working relationships with specific people. Your versatility as a performer will allow you to be more things to more people, but that does not mean you have to be everything to all people. Broadway director Philip Wm. McKinley describes this well:

*The business oftentimes likes to pigeonhole people because it makes it easier. It's not a prejudice thing. It is a way of keeping people straight in your head; "Oh, this director does this," or "This actor is a musical theatre actor and this actor is a straight play actor." If you are a multifaceted performer, it may be that you are multifaceted but specific for certain people. To some people you may be a musical theater performer. To others you may be a dramatic actor. And to another group you might be a choreographer. What is difficult is when you want to be all three of those things to everybody. It doesn't diminish your talent to be a certain type of performer or artist to different sects of producers or directors. You don't have to be everything for everybody. You can be something special for certain people. That's what I have learned in the past 20 years. There are people who deal with me as a director of spectacle; there are people that deal with me as a director of straight plays; there are people who deal with me as a master class instructor; there are people in L.A. who deal with me as a TV and film developer. There is another sect who deals with me in directing circus. I worked as a performer with New York City Opera. For the guy who owns the circus, that doesn't matter to him. That is not a talent he is looking for. So why try to impress him with that if he is not going to be impressed with it? It doesn't matter. That's the secret: What are they looking for? Don't try to impress everyone with multiple levels. Impress them in the level they are seeking.*

**Clear and timely communication is essential.** As you develop your working relationships, make sure you maintain honest communication. Express your interest in a project only if you are truly interested. If a director or choreographer is going to bat for you to be cast in a particular project, follow through. Bring your best work—don't blow off the audition when someone else is trying to get you a job and his/her reputation is on the line. It might seem crazy to have to point this out, but young performers make this mistake and they make it often without realizing it. And, of course, if a trusted colleague hires you and you need to turn the job down for any reason, make sure that person doesn't hear the news from anywhere else but directly from you first. Common courtesy goes a long way. Without it, bridges are easily burned—that person may choose not to hire you again.

Eric Sean Fogel, a choreographer for companies like Glimmerglass Opera, Washington National Opera, L.A. Opera and associate choreographer for national tours of *Happy Days*, *Little House on the Prairie*, and Broadway's *Everyday Rapture*, began his career as a dancer with the Metropolitan Opera Ballet and in musicals.

> *It always surprises me how quickly casting can happen and how often young performers miss an opportunity for taking too long to respond. When they are looking for a replacement or to fill a last remaining spot, people like to seal a deal quickly. In 2004, I was in a morning dance company rehearsal when I was left a voicemail about an offer to join the* Thoroughly Modern Millie First National Tour. *I decided to think about it for a while—what would my life be like on tour?; did I want to leave New York at that moment?; etc.— and didn't call them back until much later in the day. By the time I responded, they informed me that the former Broadway swing had expressed interest in going on tour so they had given him the contract since they hadn't heard back from me. I lost a national tour for overthinking it. Even now, I am trying to cast a featured dance role for Glimmerglass as we lost the previous performer last minute. Five days ago I reached out to six people given to me as recommendations—and I only heard back from one of them. Obviously, he got the job offer.*

**Your relationships with other performers are important.** There is a kind of camaraderie that happens in a dressing room that doesn't happen in most other professions. The people who can relate the most to the rigors that a professional faces on a daily basis are the people who are experiencing the same thing. We help each other. We inspire each other. We downright love each other. And we all go through ups and downs and rely on one another when times get tough. If you expect to have a support system, you must also *be* a support system. It isn't only about you all of the time—everyone is pounding the pavement. Everyone is putting himself or herself out there. Everyone is making sacrifices. And, everyone wants to book a job.

You will inevitably find yourself in a situation where you and a friend (or acquaintance or former castmate) are in the same final callback, possibly up for the same role. Is it a bloody battle to victory? I suppose being competitive with those around you is one way to approach it, but regardless, only one of you will get the show and the other won't. As a professional, you should absolutely present yourself at your best and try to book that job. Do the work you were trained to do and don't sabotage your own performance. But there are many factors that go into casting and, if you have been paying attention in previous chapters, you know the decision doesn't necessarily come down to "who is the most talented" or "may the best man win." It's not a talent contest. Though you are essentially "competing" for a job, it doesn't need to be about a winner and a loser. Remember that the other people in the room are your colleagues, and at the end of the day you are in the same boat. You all know what rejection feels like.

When you don't book the job, it isn't fair to direct your anger or judgment toward the person who did. They didn't book the job to spite you. They are not an enemy. No one "deserved" the job more than another. We *all* need to work. Is it fair for you to feel disappointed? Absolutely. And you will process that feeling of rejection in a constructive way. At the same time, someone you know and respect booked a job. You know the amount of work and preparation that takes. Be happy for them. Their hard work paid off and they get to do what they love to do. Know that your time will come too if you stay in the game. Showing your support for other artists in the room, as opposed to judging the other artists in the room, is a healthy way to keep positive energy surrounding you. The energy you put out there is the energy you will receive back. Celebrating each other's successes, attending each other's shows or screenings, and finding inspiration in each other's talent is what unites us as a community. In the end, it all comes down to the good old Golden Rule: treat others the way you wish to be treated!

Barry Pearl is best known for playing the character "Doody" in the feature film *Grease* opposite John Travolta and Olivia Newton-John. Across his accomplished career, he has also appeared in more than 35 television series, acted in feature films, and played leads in musicals on Broadway and national tours. He has worked with "everyone," and I think he sums it up so well.

*One asks, what is a professional? It has nothing to do with being paid; it has nothing to do with having an agent; it has nothing to do with being a union member. I know several well-paid, well-represented union members who are jackasses. It boils down to this and this alone: being professional is about how you behave at the audition and, most certainly, in the workplace. Behave. Work hard. Do your job. Maintain your integrity by using your natural-born instincts. Be honest. Be nice to everyone you work with from the ushers to the stage crew, the grips to the makeup folks. And remember the audience. Without them, there would be no medium.*

# Chapter Eight

---

# Life Happens
# (and other helpful tips)

Full-time employment as a performer is great when it happens, but it doesn't always happen and you will inevitably have "down time." These in-between times don't mean you are closed for business—in fact, it is a chance for you to concentrate on continuing your education and living your life. This business side is easy to get wrapped up in so much that you lose yourself and perhaps some of your passion for the art form. You can choose not to live that way—don't neglect to live your life outside of work! Here are some things you should learn about for peace of mind.

## SURVIVAL JOBS

During your down time, you'll need some sort of employment to still have money coming in. We call these survival jobs. Michelle Dyer, an Equity actress herself, created a website and an e-book series called *Survival Jobs for Actors* when she realized the need to ease the process for performers to secure employment between gigs. Www.survivaljobsforactors.com features national job boards, a blog, success stories and links to purchase e-books containing city-specific job listings.

Michelle describes several common types of survival jobs that performers are well suited for. These jobs offer varying schedules and tend to be positions that are easy to walk away from when the performing gigs come up. Jobs Michelle recommends seeking out include:

✓ Restaurant Industry: waiting tables, bartending, hosting
✓ Catering: private events through a service
✓ Coat Check: theaters, restaurants, clubs
✓ Promotional Gigs: handing out free samples or brochures
✓ Office Temping: requires basic office and computer skills
✓ Babysitting: for private families or through a service
✓ Personal Training or Yoga/Pilates Instructor: must get certified
✓ Be Your Own Boss: selling for Mary Kay, Shaklee, or Beachbody
✓ Retail/Sample Sales: through a specific store or a temp agency
✓ Ushering: theaters, stadiums

**What is the most important thing to keep in mind regarding survival jobs?**

MD:    *FLEXIBILITY!!! I see way too many people get caught in a job that they have to work just to make rent, and then they can't go on auditions because they have to be at work. Sometimes actors get caught in working the night shifts of their survival jobs, are then too tired to go audition, and then lose sight of why they started this career in the first place. It's a vicious cycle. Promo gigs, catering, and temp work are great, because jobs come one at a time, and you can choose to accept the job or not if you have an audition that day. Babysitting is great because it's usually in the evening. The "Be Your Own Boss" type of jobs allow you to work anywhere at any time, which is just ideal. If you are not a fan of working with the public, you probably would be better suited temping in an office and filing or stuffing envelopes. If you love meeting new people, you'll probably like working at a promotional company. It's okay to sign up with different companies. I was registered with five temp agencies, but only one or two sent me out on work. Cast your net wide and see what works for you. And be completely honest with your employer.*

**What do you do about your survival job once you book a performing gig?**

MD:    *Hopefully you started out the relationship honestly, so you will be able to tell your employer that you need those weeks off, or you'll need to leave the job. Never burn any bridges by just not showing up. Tell your employer as soon as you find out that you'll need to leave your job, and hopefully if they are able, and your relationship is good, you might be able to work with them again when you get back. Promo companies, catering companies, and temp agencies are completely used to this.*

I highly recommend you check out Michelle's website and publications.

Besides the obvious, and sometimes tedious, routine of pounding the pavement in search of these jobs, word of mouth and personal recommendations from friends are an excellent way to secure work. You should use your business style resume, as opposed to your performance resume, when applying for these jobs.

Many performers in L.A. and New York, as well as smaller markets, sign on with specialized casting agencies to work as background extras in feature films and television series. Background extras are essential to creating the realistic world the story requires. Some performers make a career working in background and even earn union status and benefits this way. Others use it as a means to earn a paycheck between larger gigs and an opportunity to learn and network. There are times an extra can receive a bump up if asked to do something featured. The hours can be long and the day rate can be minimal, but there is no better way to learn about how a set operates than by actually being on set. It is not an easy job—extras are not always treated as well as they should be; however, it is important that you maintain your professionalism regardless. A quick Google search will provide you with local casting offices that specifically seek actors for background work.

When it comes to survival jobs, you need to plan ahead. Not knowing where your next paycheck will come from can affect your mental and physical health. Accept that you will have to be diligent to achieve financial security, but know that it's possible.

# ʼERSONAL FINANCES

performing artists to rake in the dough when they first
mart about your finances. Perhaps you will be the
exception aᵢₗ_ ⱽill book something with a huge salary right off and never
have to look back. Don't make the financial assumption that it will happen
that way, however. Realistically, you should consider the following:

✓ Make the best financial decisions you can. Don't live beyond your
means. Save when you can. Learn the ins and outs of
unemployment insurance in your state before finishing a contract.
Know the minimum amount of money you need to survive each
month and budget carefully. Living in big cities is expensive, and
money will fly out of your pocket before you know it.

✓ Living off your credit cards is a bad, bad idea—this is an easy trap
to fall into and it is sometimes difficult to avoid. Though racking
up debt might seem easy in the moment, it will make your life
much more stressful down the road. Eventually, you need to pay
the money back with interest or face bankruptcy. Getting and
staying out of debt is one of the best gifts you can give yourself.

✓ Don't neglect paying on your student loans, even if you pay the
minimal amount each month. Work that payment into your
monthly budget. Putting off repayment and accruing more interest
can come back to haunt you later on, so work out a realistic plan
for yourself. Keep in mind that maintaining some savings is
important for those periods when you are underemployed, so be
mindful not to dig yourself into a hole when you need money to
survive on.

✓ When you do book a job, especially one out-of-town, look at your
financial options. Leaving town may mean giving up your survival
job. Without an immediate income source to return home to, save
money from your new job to live off of for a while when you
return home. Many performers sublet their apartments to other
industry professionals while away. Since your employer will likely

cover your out-of-town living expenses, you can save from having to spend money on your apartment back home. Be wise in how you find subletters, negotiate the terms clearly and carefully, consider the legalities of your lease, and communicate fully with your roommates. Remember, they will have to live with whomever you find. Using Facebook, Twitter, union bulletin boards, and your network are great ways to find a subletter.

✓ Be mindful about saving your receipts or bank and credit card statements. Documenting the expenses that qualify under the IRS code to reduce your tax bill means more money in your savings at the end of the year. Auditors (and most accountants) don't like it when you "just guess."

✓ Consult a financial planner if you need to, or read some financial self-help books (Suze Orman worked for me!) Find and use a realistic financial plan, even if it is only month-to-month, and stick to it. Being responsible and meticulous with finances is an important part of survival and living a healthy lifestyle.

# MAKE YOUR OWN WORK

When you find yourself in a professional drought and the work is just not pouring in, and we all do, you must reinvigorate yourself. Remind yourself that you are an artist, first and foremost. You have the freedom to create your own projects.

*It's important to stay positive, set goals, and stay active. By creating your own work, whether it's doing a cabaret or shooting sketch comedy with friends, you will feel fulfilled by having a creative outlet.*

**-Lauren Molina, Broadway star, Helen Hayes Award winner, and star of a self-produced web series**

Put together a cabaret performance singing the songs you want to sing. Choreograph a showcase of your own inspired work. Get a group of friends together and do a reading of a classic play in your living room. Go sing at a piano bar. Volunteer to assist a teacher in class. Star in your own short film. Create a funny YouTube character (wisely). Take an art class. Put together or perform in a benefit performance for a cause you believe in. Write your own songs. Write a play or screenplay using situations from your own life. Write a book. Study photography to enrich your artistry—if you become really good at it, you might discover you can make a side business out of it.

You never know what your creativity might lead to. Consider L.A.-based actress and commercial dancer Nura Awda's experience:

*My first professional job was a New Year's Eve show in a small city near my hometown. I was 17 years old and got together with three other friends to choreograph a 20-minute show just for fun. We showcased it all around the city and one day got a phone call. We were suddenly booked for 13 performances at a theater. The people around us were very encouraging and the theater was always full. It was an amazing experience for us!*

Sometimes just changing the artistic environment around you can change the energy you bring into the audition room, even if you aren't conscious of it. Artists need to create. You may or may not actually perform any of this work for the public, but the process for an artist is just as important as the product or performance. *The Artist's Way* by Julia Cameron should be on your must-read list. It will give you more tools for staying in touch with your inner artistry and finding new sources of inspiration.

# I CAN'T DO THIS ANYMORE!!!

You will cry. It doesn't matter who you are, this business will make you cry. It will happen. You will get to the bitter end and then not book the job. You will screw up in an audition. You will book a job that gets canceled. You won't be able to get seen for your dream job. You'll get cut from an audition you flew across the country for. You won't get the role you wanted, and so on…. And sometimes, disappointment will hit you hard when you least expect it and you will cry—maybe even in public if you're *really* lucky! Artists are emotionally connected people, and our passion for our art form is great. Sometimes rejection really hurts. The important thing is not that something made you cry (let it out!), but how you proceed afterwards. This business is hard. Tears alone are not a reason to give up.

## TAKING A BREAK

Sometimes the pressures of trying to survive in a crazy, unsure industry can become so overwhelming that a person becomes depressed and too unhappy to function normally. It happens. If you need to take a little break, it's okay to take a little break. Taking a break is not the same thing as giving up. If you really just want to spend six months working at your restaurant and going to class without attending any auditions, you can do that. This journey is different for everyone. In the end, it truly takes persistence to achieve, but your success is not for someone else to define. Your definition of your own success is what matters. If you take a short break, reevaluate your strategies, and come back reenergized and ready to attack your career head on, then good for you. That break gave you what you needed. If you take a break, reevaluate your career, and decide to do something else with your life and not return to performing, then good for you. That break gave you what you needed. Follow *your* journey.

## YOU DON'T HAVE TO DO THIS FOREVER

*Just as the dance you set out to choreograph may not be the dance you wind up with, the career you plan and dream about may not be the path your life takes you on. Listen to intuition. Success is a journey—not a destination.*

-Seán Curran (artistic director for Seán Curran Company; choreographer for the Metropolitan Opera and *James Joyce's The Dead* on Broadway)

The definitions of "success" or "failure" are up to you. Many people have come before you who danced or performed as younger adults and then decided to change course in their lives. Priorities can change; passions

.ests can change. There aren't many adult bodies capable of
.·. There are many who seek financial stability that acting
provide. Some people want to raise their children in a
suburv.. za outside of New York or Los Angeles. As you are deciding
whether or not to pursue the performing arts professionally, you have no
way of knowing where life will lead you in the next 20 years. Don't worry
about it. If you decide to leave the business one day, it doesn't mean you
have "failed" as a performer, unless you yourself decide you have "failed"
as a performer. If you spent five years and grew as an artist, met interesting
people, nurtured a passion, performed with joy, and had nights in a show
where your heart soared, yet you never once touched a foot on a Broadway
stage, well, that still sounds pretty successful to me. But that's me.

Should you decide to change course after performing, never fear—
there are a lot of options for someone with a background in the performing
arts, both in and out of the business. Organizations that specialize in
helping performers make that transition, notably Career Transitions For
Dancers (www.careertransition.org) and The Actors Fund
(www.actorsfund.org), assist all types of performers in discovering where
else their skills might lead them.

The entertainment business is a big business, and there are a multitude
of other jobs related to the performing arts. Actors tend to take the
spotlight because they are generally the most visible; however, they would
be standing naked on a dark stage with nothing to say or do if it weren't for
a host of other entertainment professionals. Many performers transition
into other jobs within the entertainment industry. Some focus more on the
creative side while others relate to the business side. All are necessary to
keep our multibillion-dollar industry in existence. As a side note, you don't
necessarily have to begin your career as a performer to pursue any of these.

## CREATIVE JOBS

- **Director or Choreographer**: Some performers begin assisting to
  learn the creative craft of directing or choreographing. Even if you
  aren't looking to create a show on Broadway or a feature film, there
  are theaters and producers in every market who need creative
  teams. Many of these are union jobs. High school and community

theaters and schools across the country need talented creative teams as well. Opportunities to create are plentiful.

- **Design**: Costumes, scenery, lights, sound, set decoration, property and video/projection design, etc., are all very specialized fields and may require you to go back to school for specific study.

- **Resident Director/Choreographer**: After a creative team opens a long-running show, producers may put a resident in charge to oversee the production, maintain the artistic integrity, cast and train replacements, and keep the production looking fresh. Assistants and associates may find their way into these jobs.

- **Teacher**: Whether you pass the art form on to others by teaching at a university, in a dance studio or at a conservatory, becoming a good teacher can be a rewarding career. Giving back to the next generation is an age-old art form in itself.

- **Writer:** The person who can dream up the story in the first place is the most important. Someone must have the vision to create the play, the musical, the screenplay, the television pilot, the production show, etc. Writing is a very special calling.

## BEHIND-THE-CURTAIN JOBS

- **Casting:** Having an eye for talent and matching talent to specific roles is an important part of the creative process and requires people who understand the fundamentals of training and recognize the big picture.

- **Crew Positions:** Dressers, hair and makeup, board operators, carpenters, technical directors, production managers, grips, ADs, production assistants (PAs), etc., are all vital to making successful films, concerts, and theatrical productions. These are often union jobs even if the performers are working non-union.

- **Stage Manager**: If you like to be organized, problem solve, have an eye for the big picture, and are good with people, this could be a job to explore. Stage managers and ASMs are essential to the success of a show. These can be union positions.

## ADMINISTRATIVE JOBS

- **Agent, Talent Manager, or Entertainment Lawyer**: Helping other performing artists achieve their goals can be rewarding and lucrative.

- **Arts Administration**: There are not-for-profit theater and dance companies, schools, conservatories, and other arts-related programs that hire administrative support staff with creative backgrounds.

- **Booking/Presenting**: Sometimes in-house and sometimes private, these positions are responsible for booking shows into performing arts centers, movie theaters, and clubs.

- **Company Management**: The "human resources" department of theater is a great fit for people who are organized, good with numbers, and good with people.

- **Development:** Not-for-profit companies need people to fundraise, write grants, create galas, and generate financial ways for the arts to happen.

- **Managing Director or Line Producer**: The person in charge of the finances and budgeting for a theater company or film keeps the artists creating within their means. A financial background may be a prerequisite.

- **Marketing and Public Relations**: Graphic designers with performance backgrounds create logos, posters, movie trailers, magazine ads, etc., for films and theatrical productions. There are also people who organize the events and press releases that get films and shows into the media.

- **Producing/Artistic Directing**: The person who brings together an author and a creative team with funding is vital to creating work. Some producers are charged with the task of finding investors for new commercial shows and independent films.

## JOBS OUTSIDE THE PERFORMING ARTS

There is no rule that says you have to stay in the entertainment industry. It's a big world out there. Many successful performers leave the business after a period of time to pursue completely different industries.

Christine Townsend began her professional dance career right out of high school. She danced across the globe on cruise ships and moved to New York City to pursue her dreams. After several years working professionally, including teaching at Broadway Dance Center, Christine decided to pursue another childhood dream—becoming a doctor. After going back to school for her bachelors degree, she recently completed her second year of medical school.

> *The dance training I received growing up instilled a strong sense of discipline in me that is extremely helpful now in medical school. Studying for 10 to 12 hours in a day is a common occurrence, and I believe that the discipline I've learned from dancing has helped me to be successful with managing such an intense schedule. Performing, specifically, helped me to be more confident and outgoing and develop a better bedside manner. I often have patients comment on my ability to talk to them and make them feel more comfortable. The physicians that I am working with are confident in me as a student.*

Troy Edward Bowles had a successful performance career that spanned Broadway (*Chitty Chitty Bang Bang, The Pirate Queen*) and national tours (*Movin Out, Mary Poppins*) as well as feature films, theme parks, cruise ships, summer stock, television, and dance companies. After checking many performance goals off his "bucket list," Eddy decided to change course in his life and start a new chapter. He moved from New York City to Denver and now owns a successful small business.

*I met my partner, David, while touring through Denver with the First National Tour of* Mary Poppins. *He is a photographer, and when brainstorming what I could do in Denver we decided that opening a custom framing shop to go with David's photography studio would be a good fit. I applied for a grant through Career Transitions for Dancers that paid for my training. Now that I own my own business and have to do consultation with clients on design for their pictures or art, I notice that it really is like an audition. I have one chance to make an impression and sell the client on the product, which now just happens to be custom framing rather than my performance. After years of auditioning, I know that even a "fake it till you make it" approach is helpful. Trying to incorporate yourself into the design yet please the client is like making sure that you show the choreographer or casting director who you are through your performance yet remain true to the actual choreographic style. I still get nervous when someone walks in the door with some art to frame, but after years of being in auditions I know to breathe and focus and not let the nerves show.*

Jonathan Corella-Sandler graduated Magna Cum Laude from Columbia University with a bachelor of arts in dance before spending several years as a New York performer. He appeared on Broadway in *Mary Poppins* and *Wicked*, performed on national tours of *Sweet Charity* and *Doctor Dolittle*, and recorded an album of his original music that he performed live across the country. In his late 20s, he left his performing career behind when he entered Loyola Law School. Jonathan is now an attorney living in Los Angeles with his husband, Joseph, also a dancer on Broadway and in television. I asked him if he regretted waiting to go to law school.

*I knew that I was capable of doing something aside from performing, and I always intended in the back of my mind to have a professional degree. It happened exactly when it was meant to happen. I am glad I pursued my dreams first. No regrets. And going to law school was like reaching for a whole new set of dreams that way, not doing something "safe." Now I can make the arts something I enjoy again on my terms.*

Dexter Foxworth moved to Orlando to perform on an Equity contract at Walt Disney World after earning a BA in choreography from a small liberal arts college in South Carolina. While still performing full-time, he earned a BS in organizational management and as well as his MBA.

Sidelined by an injury, Dexter made the transition into the management side of production, eventually becoming a producer for Walt Disney Entertainment and overseeing shows for the parks and cruise line. Two years ago, he left show business altogether to become the executive director of a non-profit, The Zebra Coalition, which assists displaced LGBTQ youth in central Florida. Dexter always knew he wanted to perform only a short time in his life before moving on to different things. While fulfilling one dream, he was able to work toward attaining the necessary training required to fulfill another. The skills he developed as a performer continue to serve him as a businessperson.

*Discipline is key to any performer's success. Career, education, even recreational activities move ahead when discipline comes into play. Every successful professional in the world has adopted this tool. Discipline equipped me with the proper tools to be a successful professional for a Fortune 500 company and now as an executive for a non-profit. As a performer you have to maintain incredible focus in the studio and during a performance. I come to my job focused and ready to work every day; ready to tackle any obstacle. Always improving and growing, performers are constantly pushing themselves to get stronger and be better than their last performance. With any job, you have to have that same focus. You must continually work to improve by reading, learning new skills, and educating yourself. Success in anything requires an unwavering level of dedication. Approach life with discipline, and you will get wherever you wish to go.*

A life in the arts only limits your future possibilities if you allow it to. Possessing the strength, determination, and bravery to pursue your passion, however long you pursue that journey, will only add to your future success.

## Chapter Nine

# Directly From the Pros

Real people with successful careers in show business began like you— they had passion and a dream. Whether from a small town or big city, people just like you "make it" in show business every day. We all experience setbacks and steps forward, disappointments and rewards, mistakes and triumphs, but through it all passion remains the driving force. We all remember what it was like to be where you are right now—young, hopeful, and full of every possibility.

## ADVICE, ENCOURAGEMENT, AND WORDS OF WISDOM

This chapter features several industry professionals, their stories, and the words they hope you'll take to heart. Each person here found personal success through common denominators: They got the right training, put themselves out there over and over, worked hard, found their niche, and still continue to thrive as artists working at the top of the field. They were not afraid to take the plunge when it counted and follow the path they were meant to follow.

---

**Head down the professional path for the right reasons.**

The business is hard, fame is uncommon, and success can mean many things. If you aren't being driven by pure passion for the art, perhaps you should really think about whether or not this is for you.

---

**Constantine Maroulis** grew up in New Jersey, trained at the Boston Conservatory and Williamstown Theater Festival, and starred as "Roger" in the non-union tour of *Rent* all prior to achieving national fame on *American Idol*. After the show he recorded and toured as a rock singer and later was Tony-nominated for his portrayal of "Drew" in *Rock of Ages*. He continues to work as a lead on Broadway and national tours, and is a frequent guest star on television series and talk shows.

> *The goal of winning a TV reality show in order to begin your career is not the answer, unfortunately. People are going to read this and might say well, yeah, but look at you. But, look at me—first I put in the work. I went to school. I did summer stock and a tour.* American Idol *just happened at the right time in my career. It could have turned out differently, but I would have kept working either way. We are in such a celebrity-obsessed society that kids want it all too fast—it's not going to happen that way. You can't do this just to be famous. You have to do it because you love it and need it. You have to do it because the work is the only thing in your life you feel so passionate about.*

**R. Kim Jordan** was an associate to Broadway choreographer Larry Fuller, helping to set and supervise companies of *Evita* all over the world. She is currently a vice president of Actors' Equity Association and directs and choreographs for cruise ships.

> *You don't have to like all aspects of the industry, but if you don't just love it/ sleep it/ want it/ live for it, then don't do it. It's hard to be rejected and not know why. It's hard to go from job to job and maybe not even build a career. If you can't embrace all of it, move on. There are other great careers out there.*

**Gus Kaikkonen** grew up in Michigan and made his Broadway debut in the original cast of *Equus*. Other acting credits include Tommy Tune's *Cloud 9*, *The Country Girl* on Broadway, *Law & Order SVU/Criminal Intent*, *All My Children*, and *One Life to Live*. Now the artistic director of Peterborough Players, Gus has directed countless plays and musicals for off-Broadway, regional, and university theaters.

> *What is success? Fame? Wealth? Happiness? And how do you hold onto any of it over the long term? I think in our business, just making a living counts as success. I've worked with very wealthy successful stars who are so miserable I wouldn't want their lives. Show business is very hard on the pocketbook and*

*the ego. Stay in the business if it's the only thing you can do and be happy. Once you've accepted the truth of that for yourself, it leaves you very little reason to whine, regardless of where you are in your career or your bank account. If you stay in, you know why you're doing what you're doing—because there's no other choice. I'm very grateful to have found this business—as tough as it's been— and yes, I'm happy.*

---

### Embrace opportunity.

When someone opens a door for you, don't be afraid to walk through it. Take risks. Let fate run its course. The opportunity to do what you love, and make a living doing it, is a gift—but a gift means nothing if you don't unwrap and enjoy it!

---

**William Ryall** has 13 Broadway shows, seven national tours, and several TV shows, commercials, and films to his credit. A graduate of the American Academy of Dramatic Arts, he has worked with a who's who list of directors including Hal Prince, George Abbott, Tommy Tune, Des McAnuff, Sir Peter Hall, Rob Marshall, Susan Stroman, and Kathleen Marshall. Making his Broadway debut in the 1986 hit *Me and My Girl*, Bill most recently performed on Broadway in *Chaplin.*

> *A bit of advice that stayed with me came from the "First Lady of the American Stage," Helen Hayes. Miss Hayes spoke at my graduation from acting school and her advice to us was quite simply, "Go anywhere to be on a stage. It doesn't matter where you are; if you are working at your craft on a stage you will learn something." It seems quite simple but this made a huge impact on me and informed many of my decisions about accepting work. The truth of this is that I have indeed learned as much working in a theater in Wichita as I have on a Broadway stage.*

**Mic Thompson** trained as a competitive ballroom dancer in Modesto, California. After dancing in Las Vegas casino shows, he moved to L.A. and got a survival job at a Häagen Dazs on Hollywood Boulevard. One fateful day, Debbie Allen walked in as a customer. After chatting, she offered him a job as an extra on the television show *Fame*. Mic was soon promoted to a principal dancer on the show and went on to dance with Michael Jackson in several tours and videos. Mic has created shows as a director and choreographer for casinos in Las Vegas, cruise lines, the Lido de Paris, and the Walt Disney Company.

*You'll be guided by the energy you give to others so be open to all opportunities. If someone offers you a job, take advantage of going somewhere new. Be able to look back and enjoy the experiences of visiting other cultures and meeting new people. I love that I got to travel so much. Be available to be guided to new things. The jobs aren't always going to be offered, so when you are invited to be a part of something, don't limit yourself. Go where the opportunity takes you.*

---

**Focus on the work and look at the bigger picture.**

It is easy to get caught up in the distractions, but don't lose sight of why you're here. You are building a career over the long term.

---

**Matt Lenz** was the associate director of *Hairspray* and *Catch Me If You Can* on Broadway, and the resident director for *Disney's Beauty and the Beast*. He has directed for several leading regional theaters as well as international and touring companies of *Hairspray*. He is also a teaching artist for The Broadway Dreams Foundation.

*Show up, be present, and contribute. Be the person people want to work with. I advise actors to prepare, do your absolute best, and always keep learning.*

**Jessica Walter** attended the High School for Performing Arts (the *Fame* school) and the Neighborhood Playhouse in New York before launching her career. She has worked on more than 120 different television shows as a series regular, recurring character, or guest star, winning an Emmy Award for Outstanding Actress for *Amy Prentiss*. As "Lucille Bluth" on *Arrested Development*, she also received an Emmy nomination. Her many Broadway credits include Neil Simon's *Rumors* (opposite her husband, Ron Leibman) and the 2011 revival of *Anything Goes*.

*Perseverance! If anything can stop you from doing this, you'd better let it. If you don't put blinders on, it's not going to be an easy path (if it will get you there at all). They help get you through all the rejections or being shown the door quickly in auditions. Do I still get nervous at auditions? Oh my god, yes! Luckily, I don't have to audition that often anymore, but I still do occasionally. But I use that nervousness. You can make it work for you, but you have to focus. Once you get into that waiting room, it's not a place to chitchat and catch up with old friends. You really have to focus on what it is you're going to do in that room. I learned that early on. Focus on the work.*

**Phil LaDuca** was a dancer on Broadway in revivals of *Brigadoon, Pirates of Penzance* and Twyla Tharp's *Singin' in the Rain* before he switched gears and revolutionized the dance shoe industry. He created the first flexible character heel, and as a result, has become the go-to dance shoe designer for Broadway shows, musical artist concert tours, and feature films.

*What a performer needs to realize is that whether it is their first or 2,345th performance, it is always that audience's FIRST time ever seeing it. The great Graciela Daniele passed on this trick to me: when you are in a long run, don't change choreography or staging, but do change your intentions. Play a different emotion that night (joy, jealousy, flirtatious), or dance a color (red, blue, orange). In other words, make the performance new for you every night too. If you are not willing to give it your all, every night, you are cheating the audience, your fellow performers, yourself, and worst of all, your art. If you can't bring it, get off the stage and let someone else get out there who will!*

**Wayne Bryan** began his career as a Broadway performer and eventually transitioned into directing. He is the artistic director of Music Theatre Wichita. MTW hires college theater majors to perform alongside Broadway actors in their seasons each summer and has launched the careers of several successful performers including Kelli O'Hara and Kristin Chenowith.

*If you find yourself in a performing situation that is less fulfilling than you had hoped, don't blow it off, thinking that particular job doesn't matter. People talk. People remember. Someone on that show will later become a producer, a casting director, a stage manager, or someone else with the power to put in a good word for you, or to keep you from being hired (because you were a jerk in that given situation). This doesn't mean you put up with unsafe conditions or personal abuse in a job, but try to always exhibit professionalism, no matter the situation.*

**Jay Russell** holds a BFA in acting from Syracuse University. On television, he played a recurring role on FX's *Louie* and guest starring and principal roles on *Ugly Betty*, *The Sopranos*, *Bored to Death*, *Law & Order*, *Spin City* and many more. He has played leading roles in plays and musicals off-Broadway and in regional theater. Broadway and national tour credits include *End of the Rainbow*, *The Play What I Wrote*, *Beauty and the Beast*, and *Wicked*.

> *Realize that as much as you want "this particular job," you are in this for a career and not just for the momentary glory of booking one gig. Actors say, "I had three callbacks for that show and then I didn't book it! They hated me!!" No, they did NOT hate you. You did everything you could and should have or you wouldn't have gotten three callbacks. They just went with someone else. Getting a callback is a good thing. Your career is about building fans of your work—directors, casting directors, other actors, etc.…*

**Jeremy Leiner** graduated with a BFA in musical theater from the University of Michigan. While studying, he cut his professional teeth performing in summer stock at Music Theatre Wichita and West Virginia Public Theater. After performing in his Senior showcase and signing with a talent agent, he moved to New York and soon booked the 25th Anniversary tour of Hal Prince's *Evita* followed by the First National Tour of *Bombay Dreams*. Jeremy switched gears to become a talent agent and now represents legit actors in television, film, and theater.

*This is a career about passion, drive, determination, and the product of years (and in many cases, a lifetime) of training. So many of us made the decision to do this "for the rest of our lives" when we were too young to know how long that really is. A career is a marathon with many milestones along the way. Pace yourself, stay focused and grounded, and take pride in your work. If I have learned one thing from being on the other side of the table, it is that everyone wants you to get the job. If you are in an audition room, it is for a reason and because you are supposed to be there, so do not question why. While the work you do in the room is extraordinarily personal, the outcome is a business decision and has very little to do with you. The way you conduct yourself in an audition is an indication of the person they will be working with. Be friendly, be professional, and BE PREPARED.*

**Ian Knauer** earned his BFA from the University of Michigan. After working for several years on Broadway (*Mamma Mia, By Jeeves, State Fair*), in national tours, and in regional theater, he relocated to London. He is currently working in the U.K. as an actor in both film and theater including the West End's *Dirty Rotten Scoundrels* directed by Jerry Mitchell.

*See as much theatre, film, TV, and art that you can to see what others are doing and how they are doing it. I've learned so much over the years from others and always steal from the best! But I don't imitate others. I apply what I see and put that into my own expression as much as I can. When you are starting out, find the roles that you are right for, ask others what they feel you are right for, and then start preparing for those auditions, even if they are not coming up right away. This helps you to be more focused on what you want to happen in your career.*

---

**Don't limit learning to just the classroom.**

There will be teachers and unlikely lessons all around you at all times. Continue to stay open and embrace the advice, notes, and experiences that will help you grow and achieve your potential.

---

**Seán Curran** began his professional career as a leading dancer for the Bill T. Jones/Arnie Zane Dance Company for 10 years before joining the original off-Broadway company of *STOMP*. He founded his own New York dance company, Seán Curran Company, and continues to choreograph works for major concert dance and opera companies around the world. His work in NYC has been seen on Broadway and at Lincoln Center including the Metropolitan Opera.

*As a dancer, you must remember that "discipline is freedom." Taking class daily and using different modalities such as Pilates or yoga to maintain technique and physical strength is crucial and will keep you dancing for a long time. In addition to treating your physical body intelligently, nourish your mind and spirit with as much performance and as many different kinds of theater as you can see. This will inform your choices as an artist and inspire what you do and how you do it. I like to think of my own artist self as "in a constant state of becoming."*

**John Charron,** an L.A. based director/choreographer, began his training at a young age. In his teens, he joined the international touring group *The Young Americans.* After a long career working as a performer in Los Angeles, he turned his attention to directing and choreographing. He has created well over 50 original productions for Holland America Cruise Line as well as industrials and Broadway musicals.

*The most memorable advice I got: I hate to say it, but, "Butch it up, man, butch it up!" I was a little twinkie gay boy who started working when I was 15. I had fun dancing the girl's stuff. I was cast in* The Young Americans *when one of the directors said this to me. At first, I took it terribly. It was awful. I was devastated. But I realized very quickly that it wasn't a personal judgment. It was honest advice to help me work more. It was to help me get jobs. They taught me how to be full out and step up as a male dancer. I took the advice and never stopped working.*

**Naomi Kakuk** booked the national tour of *CATS* in her last semester at the University of Utah. When that Equity tour closed to become non-union, she moved to New York. Jeff Calhoun, Casey Nicholaw, Rob Ashford, and Susan Stroman have all hired Naomi for original Broadway and touring casts, including her Broadway debut, *The Producers.* As an actress, she has appeared in dozens of national commercials. For five seasons, she has performed as a Rockette at Radio City Music Hall and can be seen as the face of their seasonal marketing campaign across the Northeast.

*Lightning has to strike sometimes to get your foot in the door, but everyone gets their start somewhere. You aren't going to come out of college ready for every job. There will be some things you are ready for right away, but your career will have a progression. Jobs you get now will prepare you for the jobs you will get down the road. I auditioned for* Contact *when I moved to New York, but I wasn't ready to play "Girl in the Yellow Dress" until much later in my career. I didn't see that at age 22. I started as a strict ballet dancer. Doing* CATS *gave me a different confidence in myself onstage—I wasn't afraid to play after that. Watch the people you work with, find what you like, and steal from the best. When I got* The Producers, *I thought I could tip [showgirl walk].*

*Then in rehearsal I watched [longtime Broadway performer] Angie Schworer tip and it looked like she invented it. That was when I really learned how to tip. Now I'm a Rockette. You can never stop learning.*

---

### Display professionalism generously.

You choose the type of businessperson you put out there. You can choose to be the consummate professional that others like to work with. That professionalism extends well beyond level of talent.

---

**Kathleen Marshall** won Tony Awards for her choreography of *Anything Goes, The Pajama Game,* and *Wonderful Town,* all of which she also directed. She has over 16 Broadway shows and three feature films to her credit. She and her brother, director Rob Marshall, began careers as young performers in their hometown, Pittsburgh. She moved to New York after graduating from Smith College and was the dance captain/swing for the national tour of *CATS* before transitioning to assisting and then choreographing and directing on Broadway.

*There are people who jump up to get paper towels when the coffee spills   whether it's their spill or not—I like working with those kinds of people. And it's the Girl Scout motto: Be prepared! You should always feel that you could walk into any audition or rehearsal completely at the top of your game.*

**Steve Saari** played piano with touring orchestras and in pits on Broadway and national tours and as an audition accompanist for Tara Rubin Casting before musical directing long-running off-Broadway musicals. He has written and performed his own shows in NYC cabaret venues and currently directs the lead singers at Royal Caribbean Cruise Line as a vocal director.

*How you talk with the accompanist matters. The people behind the table will ask the accompanist's opinion after you leave the room. Don't snap your fingers at the accompanist like he is a waiter at a French bistro. Snapping doesn't communicate the style or groove of the song. The pianist is sometimes the MD or assistant—you never know. Bring an energy into the room that communicates you are someone another person would want to work with.*

**Mark Chmiel** made his Broadway debut tap dancing alongside Patti LuPone in the Lincoln Center revival of *Anything Goes*. He also performed in the Rob Marshall revival of *Damn Yankees* and played leading roles in national tours and regional theaters across the U.S.

*I was standing with the rest of the cast, in Columbus Circle, waiting for the bus that would take me on my first national tour. For weeks, I asked every actor I saw what advice they had for the road. As a result, my bags were overstuffed with clothes for every season, a travel iron, a hotpot, and plenty of nice thick books. (As I travelled, I acquired the things I ACTUALLY needed and began to drop these packed items, like weighty ballast, from one city to the next.) But just before I loaded that bus, one more actor/friend walked by. I asked for his one piece of advice. He looked at that motor coach, thought for a moment, and replied, "Remember it's a fish bowl. It's easy to forget about the real world, and get caught up in all the backstage drama. Stay out of the drama." Well, as Noel Coward wrote, "Time and again I try. Time and again I fail." Don't YOU fail. And don't ever let up.*

**Stephen DeRosa** holds an MFA in acting from the Yale School of Drama. He has appeared on several episodes of *Boardwalk Empire* as "Eddie Cantor" and guest starred on such TV series as *Law & Order* and *Ugly Betty*. A versatile actor, his various Broadway credits include *The Nance*, *Into the Woods*, *Henry IV*, *Twentieth Century*, *Hairspray*, and *The Man Who Came to Dinner*.

*"Have fun and forget the politics." This doesn't mean don't have a passion for government or current events. The politics in this case refer to the power games that might be going on in the business of the show. They could have to do with conflicting egos, with casting, with favoritism, with money, and even sometimes (gasp!) sex—though that's a lot less than some TV shows would have you believe. In the end, just go in and try to do your job with 100% devotion and be supportive of others. Every bit of show business has a degree of political b.s. that is best to avoid.*

> ## Be full out.
>
> You are pursuing a career that requires 100% commitment on many different levels. Give it your all both on and off stage. No one else can do it for you.

**Maud Arnold** moved to L.A. at age 17 to train at the Debbie Allen Dance Academy. As co-artistic director of the DC Tap Festival with her sister Chloe, she has made a name for herself as a tap dancer as well as a commercial dancer, teacher, and assistant director of music videos. She was Beyonce's stand-in and dance double for several videos and has appeared on HBO's *Boardwalk Empire*. Maud went back to school after beginning her career to earn a degree in film from Columbia University.

> *"The way you practice is the way you perform!" is the advice I learned from Toni Lombre, my tap teacher from Washington D.C.*

**Jinger Leigh Kalin,** a renowned and skilled magician/illusionist, moved to Los Angeles after growing up in Connecticut. She met her husband, Mark Kalin, performing in a show in Guam, and they soon became a headlining magic act on the Las Vegas Strip. Their signature production, *Carnival of Wonders*, set a new standard in magic revues. They recently starred in the world tour of *The Illusionists*.

> *When it comes to performing, you can never be over-prepared. Rehearse, rehearse, rehearse! Do not assume that your audience cannot tell whether you are prepared or not. Do not insult them! When rehearsing, do it 100%. That way, with added adrenaline, your performance will always be at 110%.*

**Timothy George Anderson** is from Texas and trained under the EDGE Scholarship program in L.A. before launching a career. A great working relationship with choreographer Marguerite Derricks led to dancing roles in several feature films and television series including *Austin Powers III*, *MADtv*, and the *Billboard Music Awards* with Britney Spears. On Broadway, he performed in *The Color Purple* and *9 to 5*. A knee injury sidelined him from dance; the required physical therapy led him to a new career as a personal trainer. After touring with his client, Madonna, he helped to establish Hard Candy Fitness.

*Never wait to be full out in an audition or performance. Give 100% every time because you never know if it will be your last. As cliché as that sounds, it is very true. Also, be confident in your talents but at the same time keep your humility. Be open to criticism, evolve, and never stop learning. The world is constantly changing and so are we as humans. We keep pushing the boundaries of what is normal, what is good enough, what is beautiful, what is unattractive, what is acceptable, or what makes us happy. Change is going to happen with or without us, but I feel it's better to embrace it than fight it.*

**Janelle Abbott Staley** was a student of Grand Rapids Ballet in Michigan before earning a BFA in ballet performance from the University of Utah. She immediately moved to New York and immersed herself in the downtown concert dance scene. As a principal dancer for several companies, Janelle established relationships early on that led to being cast in music videos for Norah Jones and Elton John. She was the lead in David LaChapelle's dance film created for Elton John's *The Red Piano* in Las Vegas. Janelle now calls New Hampshire home with her husband and two daughters.

*You must be accountable to and for yourself. No one is going to hand you a career. You have to be willing to work for it. Young dancers are often unprepared for what little help awaits them once they are out of a school or a company environment. No one is going to make you take class or bring you to an audition. It will be up to you to seek out new mentors and audition opportunities. Establish relationships. Remember that every class, every audition, every rehearsal is an opportunity to learn. And be ready for the unexpected. When an opportunity presents itself, you need to be on top of your game.*

---

### Don't lose sight of "you."

You can be your own best friend and your own worst enemy, and it is easy to get caught up in trying to be whom you think they want you to be. Remember that you are your own person and an artist.

---

**Lauren Molina** began college at the University of Michigan with an undecided major before finding her way to vocal performance and eventually a BFA in musical theater. She won the Helen Hayes Award as Best Actress for her portrayal of "Cunegonde" in *Candide*. On Broadway, she originated the roles of "Regina" in *Rock of Ages* and "Johanna" in John Doyle's *Sweeney Todd*. She also toured as a backup singer in Sarah Brightman's *La Luna* world tour and performs in NYC cabaret venues with her band, The Skivvies.

> *The best advice I ever received, and that I live by, was to be myself and trust my instincts. Embracing my quirks and my special skills has set me apart and made me unique in this business.*

**Clyde Alves** moved from Canada to play "Tommy Djilas" on Broadway in *The Music Man*, winning the Astaire Award. He repeated the role in the Disney movie starring Matthew Broderick. Clyde has appeared in eight Broadway shows across his career, including *Nice Work If You Can Get It* with his wife, actress Robyn Hurder, *Bullets Over Broadway*, and *On The Town* as "Ozzie."

> *Stay humble, remember where you came from, and carry that respect with you as you move forward. People like hiring people who are easy to get along with. Having a strong sense of who you are can be very showing, and it stands out in an audition room. Having the awareness that you don't know everything and that you are not perfect will inspire you to keep learning and improving. Treat everyone with respect, and always come into every new gig like an open book, ready for new experiences and lessons.*

**Karla Garcia** was an award-winning competition dancer in Maryland. After she graduated from NYU's Tisch School of the Arts and debuted on Broadway in *Hot Feet*, she was a Top 15 finalist on *So You Think You Can Dance* Season 5. Since the TV show, Karla has appeared on Broadway in *West Side Story*, First National Tours of *Wicked* and *The Addams Family*, the Bad Boys of Dance Australian tour with Rasta Thomas, VH1's *Divas Live*, MTV's *America's Best Dance Crew*, and NBC's *Smash*. She teaches master classes across the U.S. and abroad.

> *"Stand out and be different." When I learned this, I was almost too young and immature to really grasp the concept. As I grew older, I came to understand*

*that this doesn't mean you should aim to be like someone else, or pretend to be an eccentric, crazy version of yourself just to get noticed at an audition. I learned that you just need to be who you are to the MAX. I think this sense of authenticity and honesty as a performer really shines through. As performers, we all have amazing, individual gifts to offer. It's important to stay true to yourself and your own abilities.*

**Kenway Kua** grew up in Honolulu, Hawaii. After just one year studying theater at BYU, he was hired by Disney to perform in Florida. He then worked as a commercial dancer in Los Angeles before heading to New York. Kenway made his Broadway debut in *The Frogs* and was the first replacement in *Wicked*, where he stayed for seven years. He has performed in national tours of *Flower Drum Song* and *Mary Poppins* and the pre-Broadway engagement of *Aladdin* at the 5th Avenue Theater.

*People will love you and your work, and people will hate you and your work. Be true to yourself, the craft, and the piece. Know your strengths, work on your weaknesses and be the best you. There is only one of you.*

**Linda Mugleston** studied opera at Utah State University, and upon moving to New York, she booked her Broadway debut, *On the Town*, from her very first audition. On Broadway, she has performed in the ensemble while covering stars such as Vanessa Williams (*Into the Woods*), Donna Murphy (*Wonderful Town*), Mary Stuart Masterson (*Nine*), Marin Mazzie (*Kiss Me Kate*), Megan Mullally (*Young Frankenstein*), and Victoria Clark (*Cinderella*).

*Each person is special and has something different and unique to bring to any given role. Don't be so concerned with what other people are doing. Do YOUR work.*

**Jacki Dowling Ford** grew up dancing at her mom's studio in Utah. After earning a BFA degree in ballet, she moved to New York and performed as a Radio City Rockette for three years. She and her sister have choreographed for *SYTYCD* and created their own dancewear clothing line Jo+Jax. She has taught and choreographed across the U.S., as well as Japan, and continues to work while raising her family.

*Confidence, confidence, confidence. We create it; it's not given to us by someone else (or a trophy). It's not some tangible thing. If you don't have confidence, pretend you do. If you WERE confident, how would you act? How would you approach the class/audition/interview? Start there. There's really no difference between "pretending" you are confident and actually having confidence.*

**Dante Puleio**, originally from New Jersey, didn't begin his dance training until age 19. After studying in the U.K., he finished his degree at the University of the Arts. He joined the Limón Company in 2000 and has since toured and taught with them all over the world. While on hiatus, he also performs in musical theater and commercial dance work and teaches at Steps on Broadway.

*Stay out of your own way. You know what you want, so do it. Those little voices in your head are just that...little! Give them attention and they only get bigger!*

**Ben Franklin** earned his degree from Shenandoah Conservatory before going on to perform lead roles in regional theaters, concerts at Lincoln Center, and shows off-Broadway. He and his husband founded 2 Ring Circus, a musical aerial company, and have produced original circus revues in New York, on tour, and for cruise ships and nightclubs.

*Don't get in your own way. Patience is everything. I have gone through stages in my life where I doubted myself and my abilities and it has affected my work. Don't let personal demons of wanting to be better affect your work in rehearsal, onstage, or in auditions.*

**Ellyn Marie Marsh** worked as an actress in regional theater for several years before landing her first two Broadway shows—both of which closed before she had the chance to perform in them! Her luck changed when she was cast in the original company of *Priscilla Queen of the Desert,* where she performed for the entire run. She was a member of the original cast of the Tony-winning hit *Kinky Boots* directed by Jerry Mitchell. She lives in New Jersey with her husband and daughter, Lola.

*Sometimes you're just not "right." I once had a friend lose a big job because she reminded one of the producers of his ex-wife. There are a million different things that go into casting; you just have to do your best and hope the cards fall in your direction. It's not always you. It's also not always about talent. So don't beat yourself up about it...unless you totally sucked; then, feel free to beat yourself up.*

**Nicholas Cunningham** grew up in Australia before relocating to Paris with the Moulin Rouge and then London's West End where he appeared in *Movin' Out* and *La Cage aux Folles*. As the associate choreographer, he moved with *La Cage* to Broadway and got his green card. Other credits include *The Phantom of the Opera* on Broadway, the feature film *Nine*, and international tours with The Bad Boys of Dance, The Pet Shop Boys, and Matthew Bourne's *Swan Lake*.

> *Follow your heart, be the person who you want to be, and it will happen. Believing in yourself and having a true belief in what you do is the key to success. You will find that when you walk into a room with commitment, conviction, presence, joy, passion, and light, it will reflect back into what you do. The world will repay you.*

**Roy Lightner** began performing as a teenager in Overland Park, Kansas. While earning his bachelor of music from Oklahoma City University, he performed for five summers with Music Theatre Wichita. He earned his Equity card soon after graduation, performing in regional theater, at Lincoln Center and on Holland America's world cruise. Roy is now a choreographer and on the faculty of Ithaca College.

> *Don't lose you and what you do. People move to New York or L.A. "green," meaning that they don't know what is expected of them. That doesn't mean they aren't talented or skilled. People get to the city and suddenly think they don't know anything. (Of course you don't yet know the ins and outs of everything. Duh! My first professional show I didn't know the stage manager called cues.) This insecurity can easily allow people to lose their identity. We want a job so bad that we forget to be artists. People want to hire artists. Stay an artist.*

**Kurt Domoney** earned his BFA from CCM after growing up in Denver, Colorado. He worked in major regional theaters across the U.S., the *Radio City Christmas Spectacular* in New York, and the First National Tour of *42nd Street* before making his Broadway debut in *A Chorus Line*. He cofounded Broadway Kids Auditions, a workshop program for young theater students.

> *Remain human. Allow yourself to make mistakes. I can get so sucked into perfectionism and desperation around "succeeding in the business." It's taken me years to realize that I'm allowed to have hobbies and interests that exist*

*outside of the entertainment business. We often "live to work," which is honorable, but losing yourself isn't. Don't think with scarcity, but rather look at the abundance of opportunities that are out there. Allow yourself to push the envelope and explore all parts of who you are. This will make you a dynamic performer and a beloved colleague. Remember that you're here because you're talented and it's your dream. I'm showing up for my life and my dream.*

**Anthony Wayne,** from Norfolk, Virginia, graduated from Shenandoah Conservatory and performed in non-union tours prior to earning his Equity card in regional theater. His Broadway credits include *Priscilla Queen of the Desert,* the original casts of the Tony-winning *Pippin* and *Anything Goes,* and First National Tours of *A Chorus Line* and *The Color Purple.* Anthony recently co-produced and starred in his first off-Broadway show, *Mighty Real: A Fabulous Sylvester Musical.*

*Don't forget to live. Don't get so caught up in the business and auditions and this job and the next show that you wake up one day and are 50 years old with no relationship, no children, no home, no pets, no family, and none of the joys of life that are a part of being human. You might have had a great career but you have no one to share it with.*

---

**Staying in the game is half the battle.**

We live in a world where we are conditioned to expect instant gratification. Technology is great in many ways, but a career as a performer may not evolve as quickly as you can snap a selfie on your iPhone. Persistence, patience, and perseverance will serve you.

---

**Peggy Hickey** grew up in Sacramento, California and worked as an opera and musical theater dancer before becoming a choreographer. Based in Los Angeles, she choreographed the feature film *The Brady Bunch* and television's *90210, Samantha Who, Hot in Cleveland, General Hospital,* and *Hart of Dixie.* She is a resident choreographer at L.A. Opera, and choreographed Broadway's Tony-winning hit *A Gentleman's Guide to Love & Murder.*

*Don't give up! Persistence is the largest ingredient in any success story. Someone who has built a career, a business, a life, they will tell you it is about being persistent. Even when you feel terrible, can't put one foot in front of the other, or feel there is no sense in going further, you have to keep going. I was never the best dancer; I was never the star of the show. But I worked, and I got better and better and better until one day I did get the lead. One day I did command a higher fee. You can't give up.*

**Amy Bodnar** began as a ballet dancer in Pittsburgh, but found her way to musical theater early on in her professional career. She has performed lead roles on Broadway, including "Laurie" in Trevor Nunn's *Oklahoma!* and "Evelyn Nesbit" in *Ragtime*, in several national tours, and off-Broadway. She continues to play leading roles in major regional theaters across the country.

*The best advice I ever received and have never forgotten was from my father. He used to drive me an hour to and from ballet class six days a week. One day after class I was particularly upset, and when I shared with him that I felt I was very far behind the other girls in technique and often didn't understand the combinations, he told me that I could be sure that if I didn't understand something, there was at least one other person in the room who didn't understand it either. He encouraged me not to be afraid to ask a question respectfully. And in that same conversation, he told me that if I just kept trying, working hard, and kept going to class and didn't quit, I would watch the other girls that I held in such high esteem drop out one by one. He was right about all of it.*

**Tracie Stanfield,** from a small town in Texas, grew to become a popular jazz and contemporary teacher at New York's famed Broadway Dance Center. As a choreographer, her work includes both concert and commercial works. She founded her own dance company, Synthesis Dance Project, and has taught across the United States, Japan, Mexico, Costa Rica, Turkey, Canada, Argentina, and Brazil.

*Eventually, someone will be looking for what you have to offer, if you "offer yourself" to the work. Before going to an audition ask yourself what you can bring to the work, the role, the show. Don't assume that because you have great technique that you deserve the job. Ultimately, it is about what you give, not what you get. Be generous, be nice, go to ballet!*

**Pamela Bob** received her BFA from CCM and the Oxford School of Drama. After playing lead roles for over a decade in regional theater, summer stock and workshops of new musicals, she took over the role of "Clarice Starling" in *Silence! The Musical* off-Broadway. She made her Broadway debut in *A Gentleman's Guide to Love & Murder* understudying and performing the two leading roles.

*I was doing a show that was supposed to be produced. It was all happening. Yes! And then...it just fell through the cracks. This was supposed to be my "big break." Nope. I was devastated, and went to the director for some slight coddling and patching up of wounds. To my surprise, instead of being the warm and gushy support I was seeking, he was really matter-of-fact about it. He looked at me and said, "You know what your problem is? You think life is fair." Of course, I started sobbing. Then he looked at me and said, "Just keep going." It is now 10 years later, and after experiencing a lot more "big breaks" falling through, I realize that this business is a lot of "not fair." It takes a village to get that show produced, that person cast, that director booked—and it has so much to do with luck and timing and chance, which is totally out of our control. I know that now and constantly remind myself to JUST KEEP GOING. Other things will pop up; other opportunities will present themselves. Just Keep Going. Just. Keep. Going.*

**Denny Paschall** moved to New York after a year of college. He performed in regional theater, summer stock, and the *Radio City Christmas Spectacular* tour before landing an ensemble role in *Disney's Beauty and the Beast* on Broadway. Denny was in the original cast of *Shrek the Musical* and is currently performing in *Chicago* on Broadway while he and his wife, actress Haven Burton, raise their son in New York.

*Don't let fear get the best of you. We are all afraid. Success comes from being able to harness that fear into something useful. If you really want to do it you can. There is a job for everyone in this business. Hang in there and go for it— you don't want to say, "I wish I had tried..."*

**Shanna Vanderwerker** grew up in Maryland, earned a degree from Point Park University, and worked for Walt Disney World before she moved to New York. She dance captained for tours and regional theater, eventually landing her Broadway debut as a vacation swing in *Wicked*. After that contract ended she experienced a prolonged period of unemployment.

About to leave the business, Shanna was offered the dance captain/swing position in *Wicked*'s First National Tour where she remained for five years. She and her husband, actor Justin Brill, now make their home in Chicago.

*My good friend, Christopher Gattelli, told me when I was at my wit's end working in an office and performing in free showcases just for the exposure, "It's a means to an end. Don't give up." I'm so glad I listened to him and didn't give up, or I wouldn't be where I am today. We spend more of our time unemployed and trying to get to the next job—everything will pay off in the end.*

**Wes Veldink** is from Grants Pass, Oregon, but in his teens, he moved to California to attend the Orange County High School of the Arts. In L.A., he danced in the Disney feature film *Newsies* and with Michael Jackson, Ani DiFranco, and Paula Abdul. He has taught and choreographed concert pieces around the world. Currently Wes resides in New York where his recent work includes Alicia Keys' *Set the World on Fire Tour*, the feature film *Country Strong* with Gwyneth Paltrow, and commercials for Joe Fresh.

*Honor the journey and see the bigger picture for yourself and your career. Want more. Dream bigger. Live your experience from the inside out. You aren't at the mercy of an agent's approval or a producer saying "yes" at an audition. Make decisions and choices that steer your career the way you imagine for yourself. If you find the work you want to do, you can do it, but remember it's a journey that is always evolving. There isn't a finish line.*

---

**You are a part of something much bigger.**

We are a community of artists. We create something that wasn't there before. We inspire the world. Your contribution as an artist makes our community that much stronger. You are one of us—with that comes responsibility.

---

**Justin Brill** attended Carnegie Mellon University after growing up performing in community theaters in Annapolis, Maryland. He has played lead roles in *Rent, All Shook Up,* and *High Fidelity* on Broadway, as well as national tours, Las Vegas, and regional theater. He also toured as "Boq" alongside his wife, Shanna, in the First National Tour of *Wicked.*

*We are part of a tradition of storytelling. We add to the long history of people whose life's work was to entertain. Our livelihood is only possible through the groundwork of the many generations of storytellers that came before us. No matter what heights you aspire to, always respect the work and dedicate your honest and heartfelt work to the great tradition that we are fortunate to be a part of.*

**Angel Reed** moved to Los Angeles right out of high school in Reno, Nevada. Her first professional job was playing a Muppet in *Sesame Street Live* on tour, after which she found success in television and commercials. She traveled with *Saturday Night Fever* and a European USO tour before landing a role in the original cast of the off-Broadway and subsequent Broadway musical *Rock of Ages*. She was nominated for an Astaire Award for her performance.

*Have respect for your elders and the people above you. Know where they came from. You may be the fresh new talent, but there are people who came before you and you should respect those who paved the way for you.*

**Justin Greer** earned his BFA in vocal performance and theater from Carnegie Mellon. After making his Broadway debut in *Annie Get Your Gun*, he made a career as a dance captain, swing, and understudy of leads in shows such as *Annie, The Mystery of Edwin Drood, Anything Goes, The Producers, Shrek the Musical, Seussical* and *Urban Cowboy*. He now teaches theater and dance full-time in New York.

*Be a lovely person. There are too many excellent performers, and there simply is not room in a tiny rehearsal studio for you AND your ego. Kindness toward others goes a LONG way in any business. Know that it isn't always about YOU...but be ready to make it about you when the work calls for it.*

**Richard J. Hinds** graduated from the Interlochen Arts Academy and performed in the Las Vegas company of *We Will Rock You* before turning his focus to directing and choreographing. He was the associate director for *Newsies* and *Jekyll & Hyde* on Broadway, *Here Lies Love* off-Broadway, and the First National Tours of *9 to 5* and *High School Musical*. He has directed and choreographed television specials, commercials and regional theater.

*I think it is important to remember what a small world this business is. Everyone knows everyone. Don't say or do anything you will ever regret because it will get back to someone. I just think it is important to treat everyone the way you wish to be treated. I know it sounds cliché, but it is very true.*

**Kate Hutter** opted out of high school in her Nevada hometown in favor of ballet boarding school at the Walnut Hill School. She went on to get her BFA in theatrical design from USC and her MFA in dance/choreography from SUNY Purchase before moving to Los Angeles. In 2006, she co-founded the L.A. Contemporary Dance Company, for which she is the artistic director.

*Competition can be something that drives you to attain new goals…but approach it with admiration. If there is someone who does something you love or books a job you wanted, be proud and happy, and know that is a fellow dancer and friend who achieved something great…not your arch-nemesis. Nothing was done in spite of you and your day will come.*

**Liz Pearce** moved to the U.S. as a child from the U.K. A graduate of CCM, she performed in the ensemble of national tours before landing the lead role of "Audrey" in the First National Tour of *Little Shop of Horrors*. She made her Broadway debut in *Billy Elliot*, where she understudied and performed the lead role of "Mrs. Wilkinson." Liz has also performed in the West End and plays leading roles at major regional theaters.

*"Be kind." Be kind to yourself, to the artist within you who needs taking care of, nurturing, and encouragement. Be kind to your body that you put through the ringer every night on stage. And be kind to your fellow actors and colleagues. Show them the same respect, support, openness, and professionalism that you would like to receive. In an industry that can be so harsh and challenging, a little kindness goes a long way.*

**Leslie Stevens** landed her first Broadway role at a young age when she created "Anne" in the original *La Cage aux Folles*. Based in Los Angeles, her diversity as a performer has allowed her the opportunity to appear in musicals, classical and dramatic plays, and operas as well as in guest-starring roles on TV series such as *True Blood, Private Practice,* and *The Young and the Restless*.

*There will most likely be an undercurrent of anxiety about constantly changing jobs and piecing together money as an independent contractor. You should love doing it because those are the hours/days/years of your life. Realize that someone else's success does not diminish yours. <u>Really</u> get to where you can celebrate joyous moments for others. We're all in this together—striving for excellence. If they can get to point A or B or Z, then it is also possible for you. Work your ass off, and then try to excuse yourself for your flaws. Hang with friends you trust. Look for where the cracks are, because that's where the light gets in.*

# Chapter Ten

# Take the Journey

What does it mean to "make it" in the industry? What are the definitions of "success" or "failure?" What is "the bar" a performer must achieve in order to be considered "professional"? When it comes to you and your career, no one else can define the answers to those questions but you.

Your journey as a professional performer will be your own personal journey. I wish I could say that if you just do "A, B, and C," follow my instruction manual, that I could guarantee you a successful career. But that would be a lie. No book can guarantee that because a book cannot predict the unique variables of talent and type that define you, the reader, or the unique challenges and opportunities affecting your career that only you will face. You have to use your business tools, be the best you, and take chances. Every working professional got his or her start somewhere, sought advice from others, and ventured forth by making choices and taking that chance. If you can master the business of show business, the one thing I can guarantee is that a great, fulfilling life awaits you.

Drive your ambitions. Find internal strength. Be a go-getter. No one else can do this for you but you. Always trust your instincts, be true to yourself, and pursue this for only as long as it makes you happy. Don't neglect learning from your mistakes—and realize we all make mistakes. Hopefully the knowledge you've gained and tools you've acquired from the book will prevent you from learning many lessons the hard way.

I hope you follow your dreams and I wish you a long, successful, and joy-filled life and career. Someday years from now you just might find yourself in a position where you have become the mentor to an up-and-coming performer. Embrace that opportunity—it's an honor. We are an industry steeped in tradition, and nurturing the next generation of aspiring artists is a great part of that tradition. Be generous as you pass on your expertise and advice. Give them your copy of this book—or better yet, buy them the latest edition!—and lovingly welcome them to this amazing community of which you are a part.

Oh, and don't forget to break a leg!

# Online Resource Reference

Actors Access: www.actorsaccess.com

Actors' Equity Association (AEA): www.actorsequity.org

The Actors Fund: www.actorsfund.org

American Guild of Musical Artists (AGMA): www.musicalartists.org

American Guild of Variety Artists (AGVA): www.agvausa.org

Answers 4 Dancers: www.answers4dancers.com

Backstage/Backstage West: www.backstage.com

Broadway.com: www.broadway.com

Broadway World: www.broadwayworld.com

Career Transitions For Dancers: www.careertransition.org

Dance Magazine & Pointe Magazine: www.dancemedia.com

Florida Professional Theatres Association: www.fpta.net

Gypsy's List: www.gypsyslist.com

The Hollywood Reporter: www.hollywoodreporter.com

Internet Broadway Database: www.ibdb.com

Internet Movie Database: www.imdb.com

The League of Chicago Theatres: www.leagueofchicagotheatres.com

Midwest Theatre Auditions: www.webster.edu/fine-arts/midwest-theatre-auditions

National Unified Auditions: www.unifiedauditions.com

New England Theatre Conference: http://netconline.org

Playbill: www.playbill.com

Screen Actors Guild (SAG/AFTRA): www.sagaftra.org

Show Business Weekly: www.showbusinessweekly.com

Southeastern Theatre Conference: www.setc.org

Stage Door Access/Stage Door Connection: www.stagedooraccess.com

StrawHat Auditions: www.strawhat-auditions.com

Survival Jobs for Actors: www.survivaljobsforactors.com

Theatre In _____:

    Atlanta: www.theatreinatlanta.com

    Boston: www.theatreinboston.com

    Chicago: www.theatreinchicago.com

    D.C.: www.theatreindc.com

    Los Angeles: www.theatreinla.com

    Minneapolis: www.theatreinminneapolis.com

    New York: www.theatreinnewyork.com

    San Francisco: www.theatreinsanfrancisco.com

    Seattle: www.theatreinseattle.com

Unified Professional Theatre Auditions: www.upta.org

Variety: www.variety.com

Vegas Auditions: www.vegasauditions.com

# About the Author

**Adam Cates** began his formal dance training at age eight approximately 2,688 miles west of New York City in Reno, Nevada. After performing in community theaters and dance competitions and booking some professional work as a teen, he pursued a bachelors degree in theater from the University of Utah. A longtime resident of New York City, Adam is a proud member of the Actors' Equity Association, American Guild of Musical Artists, and Society of Directors and Choreographers. He has worked as a director, choreographer, associate director/choreographer, dance captain, casting associate, swing/understudy, dancer, actor, and singer across the U.S. and abroad with credits in several mediums including Broadway, national tours, television, off-Broadway, feature film, regional theater, opera and dance companies, summer stock, industrials, cruise ships, theme parks, casinos, theater festivals, cabaret/club shows, and web series.

Adam has conducted master classes, lectures, and guest residencies for several university theater and dance programs across the United States and Canada. He is a founding faculty member of the professional performing arts high school musical theater program (PPAS) at Rosie's Theater Kids in New York and has taught for several national convention tours. Inspired by the many teachers he was privileged to study with along the way, Adam has a passion for passing on training, advice, and knowledge of the business to the next generation of professional performers.

For more, visit www.adamcates.com.

## PHOTO CREDITS

Made in the USA
Coppell, TX
02 February 2021

49372049R00134